Point of View
Talks on Education

Edward H. Levi

Point of View

Talks on Education

The University of Chicago Press
Chicago and London

Standard Book Number: 226-47412-7 (cloth)
226-47413-5 (paper)
Library of Congress Catalog Card Number: 73-101493
The University of Chicago Press, Chicago 60637
The University of Chicago Press, Ltd., London

To K. S. L.

Contents

1

The University and the Modern Condition

A talk given to the University of Chicago Citizen's Board, Chicago
16 November 1967

1

I welcome the opportunity to talk about the kind of university the University of Chicago is, the conditions of life which affect it, and the response which the university should make to the modern condition.

Quite simply and to begin with, the University of Chicago is a small university. With about 8,500 regularly enrolled quadrangle students, it is one-third or less the size of the standard unit of a single campus of a state university. Moreover, two-thirds of the students are graduate students in the graduate divisions or professional schools. With more than one thousand faculty, the faculty-student ratio is about one to eight. The College, with only 2,600 students, is one of our country's smallest top colleges; yet it has the intellectual resources of the university. The result has made it possible for Chicago over the years to be judged as one of the three universities giving the most significant leadership to the undergraduate curriculum. Between 70 and 80 percent of our undergraduate students plan to go on to do graduate work. Two-thirds of the graduate students who receive the doctorate at Chicago go into teaching. A recent survey of fifty-two universities and colleges in the East, West, and Midwest shows approximately 2,500 Chicago graduates teaching on these faculties. The professional schools—Medicine, Law, Business, Education, Social Service Administration, Divinity, Graduate Library—are centers of research. Today, as throughout its history, the university's influence is to be seen in the professions, including the profession of business, and in the universities and colleges, where Chicago is a teacher of teachers.

Some of the most important problems our country faces today are problems of mass education. A popular position holds that it is the obligation of all colleges and universities to grow to accommodate the greater numbers. Indeed, in some areas, as for example the Illinois handling of federal funds, governmental assistance for undergraduate facilities has been tied to a showing that more students will be accommodated. The University of Chicago has increased in size. Between 1954 and 1964, the student numbers grew by 18 percent: the undergraduate body went from 1,350 to 2,147—an increase of 59 percent. In the last three years the College has grown by 21 percent more. But Chicago is still small. And for the kind of university it is, smallness in size is an essential characteristic.

The university is heavily research-oriented. This is not a new development. It does not arise from the availability of corporate funds for research, the interests of the foundations, the possibility of government grants, or the desire to attract faculty. It arises because the essential purpose of the university from the start has been to discover what we can of the nature of man and his universe. A great deal of the research has been trivial. Some of it, as for example the creation of the first self-sustaining nuclear pile, has been frightening. A large part, witness the work of Dr. Charles Huggins, has been lifesaving. Much of it has rediscovered for our own time the conditions of older cultures and given us a greater awareness of our own. To the work of the scholars of our university, we owe a considerable amount of mankind's knowledge of the nature of matter, the earth, the planets, and the stars, and much of what we know—although we know too little—about the forces within our society. The first basic work in urban sociology, the widely known Chicago school in economics, the Chicago school in literary criticism, the seminal work in the learning process itself are illustrations from the humanities and the social sciences.

The decision to emphasize research was made more than seventy-five years ago. William Rainey Harper was opposed to the original idea to build only a college. "It is not a college, but a university that is wanted," he wrote. Harper wanted a college as part of a university and in the Middle West. He faced the opposition of many who felt that to combine a university with a college would be to create a "mongrel institution" which was "neither fish, flesh, nor fowl," and who thought that in any event the city of Chicago in the uneducated Middle West was decidedly not the place to put a university. Harper himself was that kind of researcher who was for that very reason an enthusiastic teacher. His plans provided at the outset "to make the work of investigation primary, the work of giving instruction secondary." This was to be implemented by making promotion of younger men "depend more largely upon the results of their work as investigators than upon the efficiency of their teaching, although the latter will be by no means overlooked." Beginning with this early statement of what is now often erroneously reduced to the label "publish or perish," Chicago has welcomed the opportunity and the strains inherent in an institution dedicated to both research and teaching.

The emphasis on research was a declaration of faith in the power of the individual mind. It carried with it a profound conviction of the importance of freedom for the mind to inquire, to know, to speak. John D. Rockefeller set the tone through a policy of noninterference. As one commentator has recently written, "No contrast could be greater than that between the early years at Stanford and the beginnings of the University of Chicago." The results in the early days showed the difference. The sharing of the new learning gave Chicago its interdisciplinary stamp and its sense of unity. It was one university. Even though Harper had all the inclinations of an empire builder, the wholeness of the university and its dedication to research evoked a concern for what was basic and not only vocational. The test was whether a new enterprise could truly contribute to the knowledge of the whole. This was the test imposed when the Law School was founded in 1902. The Law School was not to be separated either by location or by spirit from the university at large. It was to be an organic part, in close touch with the other divisions, embodying the spirit and purpose of university life and in turn contributing to that life. A scientific study of the law, it was thought even in those days when Harvard was preaching the law "pure and simple," involved the related sciences of history, economics, philosophy— the whole field of man as a social being. The same test was applied to all parts of the university. It is the reason all the professional schools are centers of research; all are interdisciplinary and all are leaders in the training for their professions.

There are two other qualities of the University of Chicago. First, the university conceives of itself as dedicated to the power of the intellect. Its commitment is to the way of reason. It stands, as Robert Hutchins said, in perpetual agreement with Cardinal Newman that the object of a university is intellectual, not moral. This is not to say that adherence to reason, the self-criticism and discipline which this imposes, does not itself partake, indeed it requires, the highest morality. Second, it must be admitted the university has a mixture of traits, lovely and unlovely, arising out of the sense of its own importance and of its uniqueness. Perhaps this is the free-swinging enthusiasm of the Middle West—a response to those who thought this was an unlikely place for a university. Perhaps this arises because the university knows that its reason for existence is to be a model of excellence. Perhaps it arises out of the confidence that those who founded the university had in the overwhelming importance of knowledge. However objectionable these traits at times may be, they have given the university its willingness to innovate, to stand alone, and to endure.

There is a problem of endurance. The university and its friends struggled greatly for its existence. The early days had their problems. Harper was tortured by the institution's financial worries. After one particularly difficult budget period, with no funds to pay the deficit, Harper, the Hebrew scholar, remarked wryly that he thought of introducing a lecture on life after death among the Hebrews since he had spent two weeks in hell and could speak realistically. He was moved in a convocation address to ask: "Do the friends of higher education in this western country appreciate what higher education costs? Do they realize that the University of Chicago, with all its millions, is not half-equipped even in the departments which it has undertaken to establish?" In each generation and in fact more frequently, the university has had to be refounded both in terms of financial resources and in its ability to pass the tests of character, will, and ability. Its dedication to freedom of thought at times has been costly. Its insistence on the basic purposes of this kind of university often has been unpopular. In our own time it waged a fight for its existence, surviving the blight of the cities from which others have fled, recreating a community into a cultural civic asset. At all times, whatever the other distractions might be, it has had to meet the test of the reality of its commitments to intellectual integrity and ability—commitments which welcome no compromise.

Our university must meet the tests imposed by the modern condition. Our society is flooded with communications. The acceptance of myths and aphorisms is not a new phenomenon, of course. But the increase in the printed word, the rise in literacy, the development of new means of communication all give rise to new burdens as well as opportunities. George Bernard Shaw had over his fireplace the motto: "They say. What say they? Let them say." Instead of this skepticism, we ask: "How often do they say it?" and "How many say it?" The test of an idea becomes the frequency with which it is repeated. This is not a test which promotes rational discussion. It is a setting in which the waves and tides of popular thought, the acceptance of a false inevitability as to points of view, the use of meretricious tests to determine truth, have magnified importance. It is a climate, and this is particularly true in matters dealing with education, where it is axiomatic that any poor idea will be catching. Popular discussion has never been enough, and it is tragic for a society if that is all the discussion there is.

Rational discussion itself is suspect. Our society is fascinated with the manipulative techniques of persuasion, coercion, and power. The sense of injustice, which all must prize, is subject to manipulation. The devastating reality and complexity of the problems to be faced, the unattainability of goals, and, tragically, even progress made—all feed the sense of injustice. The solutions call for the highest intellectual powers of man, but the excitement of victories, the frustrations of defeat, the comradeship of belonging, question these powers. The concept of reason itself appears as an artificial attempt to separate intellectual powers from the frustrations, emotions, and accidents which cause events; the concept of reason is viewed as facade to prevent change. The sense of injustice, concerned with the problems of equality, questions the standards of excellence. It asks whether the intellectual and artistic attainments of mankind —greater knowledge, discovery, skill, or understanding—have their own values and can really be separated from the culture which defines them.

Artists and writers have helped stamp upon our age the self-conception of mankind caught in a machine. This stems from a somewhat older tradition in American life. Steam and paper money were once the symbols of oppression. The implication is that man's powers will cease to be personal and choice will be gone. We have a tradition also of reciting how the wonders of science have accelerated, as indeed they have, with the implication that in a few years, if not now, life will be automatic and predetermined. The computer revolution is joined with older populist notions giving rise to new symbols, vastly helped by the Internal Revenue Service and the Social Security number. Viewing the vast powers and reach of government, the conception which emerges is of the individual caught in the grasp of a union of the welfare state, the corporate enterprise, the machines of science, and, one regrets to say, the university, which is described as a knowledge machine—a part of the educational-industrial power complex.

In a recent speech, the commissioner of education* demanded that American universities be more than centers of learning and enlightenment and more than centers of research. They must become part of the action, he said, turning "all their resources and facilities to the problem of the survival of the communities of mankind—whether the community embraces a particular localized area or a state or whether it encompasses the nation as a whole or is world wide." "The university can and must become a catalyst," he declared, "an integral element, with government and industry, in the battle for survival of the cities." He mentioned the University of Chicago. "Like the University of Chicago," he said, "encircled by increasingly decayed neighborhoods plagued with crime, juvenile delinquency, and filth, we must join in a concerted effort to rehabilitate our neighbors." He spoke

* Harold Howe II.

of the universities being great resources for these social purposes, and suggested that if the universities remain uninvolved, they could not expect the populace to give them support and freedom.

A recent letter to the *Chicago Daily News* from the secretary of the Illinois Commission on Automation and Technological Progress calls upon the educational institutions in Illinois to "concentrate now upon developing manpower resources to meet" the needs of the Weston accelerator project. For years, sociologists, economists, people who inhabit offices of education, and even fund raisers for colleges have emphasized the greater earning power of college graduates.

The uses of a university under these views then appear to be vocational and social, including as urban redevelopers, but there are other uses as well. A recent article by a political scientist from New England, repeating a hodgepodge of popular notions about higher education, suggests that the purpose of a university is to be "a kind of curiously exempt institution that our society has fortunately created, in which it is possible for people to try out a whole set of new roles, to deal with deviant behavior that the society in general would frown upon." Whatever this means, and happily it is not entirely clear, the New England professor who wrote the article makes it plain that the university should not carry on as a kind of imaginary debauch for the alumni. He appears to suggest that the university should be a series of political and social experimental communities, committed to the task of leading society into new liberal battles. The position has been taken more than once that the purpose of a university is to be in effect a launching pad for a variety of political movements. Of course the American campus cannot and should not be isolated from the kind of talk endemic to American public life. A distinguished member of the United States government in a rip-roaring speech in Berkeley recently told the students: "We get upset about four-letter words on sex, but we don't worry about four-letter words on hate, bomb, kill, maim, and guns." It is perhaps unfair to treat these remarks, intended to be a call for social commitment, as arising from a recognition that there are quite a lot of young people who are or will become voters. But the temptation to view students as an interesting resource is great.

The response of universities to the characteristics of our era must take into account the purposes of universities and the kinds of contributions they can make. Universities are among the important institutions in our society, but there are other important institutions. You will recall de Tocqueville's description: "Americans of all ages, all conditions, and all dispositions constantly form associations. They have not only commercial and manufacturing companies, in which all take part, but associations of a thousand other kinds, religious, moral, serious, futile, general or restricted, enormous or diminutive." The fact there is an unmet need does not at all mean that a university is best equipped to take it on. Even if it is, the added function may place such a burden upon an institution as to defeat its basic purposes. Even a welfare-indoctrinated society must make choices. It may be that new types of institutions are required; it does not follow that universities should become these new types. A university which claims to be all things to all people, or as many different things as different groups wish it to be, is deceitful or foolish or both.

There are of course many different kinds of institutions which are called universities. These differ enormously in size, quality, and purpose. This is true among colleges as well. Unfortunately there are great pressures upon all educational institutions to be the same, and to some extent it has become a point of honor to pretend to be the same. Instead we should be exploring the wisdom of explicit recognition of the different goals to be served, the kinds of individuality to be fostered. There is, for example, an important place for the vocational institution beyond high school. Vocational institutions ought to be further developed. If they are an essential gateway to the work of modern life, they should be available to all. There is an important place for the liberal arts college separate from a university. There is even an important place for the college which regards itself as the successor of the utopian community—an amalgam of social thought, work and rest camp, and community living. There are similar differences among the graduate and professional schools. Not all medical schools, law schools, business schools, divinity schools should be the same. Different types of institutions are deprived of their individuality and of the achievement which is possible and appropriate for them by confusion in goals and the tendency to conform. Moreover, while youth has to be wasted on the young, it is a great error to think of education as limited by age. The academy's search for knowledge and the understanding of culture should be available to all ages and is not to be confused with the problem of finding a happy home for the in-between years.

The University of Chicago began with and has achieved for itself a unique combination. Its emphasis on research is paramount. It includes within research the understanding of our own and other cultures and the appreciation of the works of the mind. It includes the search for knowledge so basic as to vastly change man's powers and comprehension. And this is not just the goal but in fact the achievement. Whatever the strains, it believes that research and teaching are closely related. Research itself—the restructuring of subject matter, the revelation of insights, new and old—can be the highest form of teaching. The obligation which the university has assumed is not only to give the individual scholar the freedom and intellectual environment required for research but to undertake to transmit the qualities and understanding of research into all of its teaching. The work in the undergraduate College proceeds with the strength of the university's search for knowledge. The recent reorganization of the College into collegiate divisions paralleling and closely tied to the graduate areas reflects this strength and this obligation. The professional schools were created for the very purpose of relating research and the responsibilities of skill and understanding to the strategic problem areas of our society. The result has given the university a special position in the whole of higher education. It is not accidental that more students from the College of the University of Chicago go on to do effective graduate work than from any similar institution, that so many of the problems of our society have been strategically identified and worked upon in a professional way at this university, and that the whole of higher education has been greatly influenced by the innovation, research, and instruction of this place.

If this appears as a paean of praise, let us admit at once there are limitations. The University of Chicago does not exist to develop manpower resources for the Weston project. It does not exist to increase the earning power of its students. It does not exist to train the many technicians needed for our society, nor to develop inventions important for industry. While it is and should be a good neighbor, it does not exist to be a redevelopment agency for the South Side of Chicago. Its primary purpose is not to be a college where students can find themselves free of the pressure of the discipline of learning. It does not exist to be a series of experimental political and social communities, nor is its institutional purpose to be found in the leadership by it of new liberal or conservative causes. I do not suppose that anyone thinks of the University of Chicago as carrying on the New England professor's imaginary debauch for its alumni. Many of these purposes may be primary for many types of educational institutions, and happily there are many. However valuable they may be for some institutions, these purposes are not primary and some of them are not appropriate for the University of Chicago. And while its faculty and students will individually respond to a variety of political and social commitments, the purpose of the university continues to be intellectual, not moral.

Perhaps, then, one should ask, "What is the service of this university?" The answer is traditional and old-fashioned. Its greatest service is in its commitment to reason, in its search for basic knowledge, in its mission to preserve and to give continuity to the values of mankind's many cultures. In a time when the intellectual values are denigrated, this service was never more required. I realize, of course, that in all this there appears to be a paradox. It is highly probable, although the subject is not a simple one, that given their choice of profession, training at the University of Chicago has increased the earning power of our students. Basic scientific work at the university could not help but have its impact upon industry. Our graduates do hold a variety of important positions in industry, in the professions, in teaching and in national laboratories. The university has been a center of self-criticism for our society. We did in fact play a major role in restoring and maintaining an integrated community, and the university's work has given leadership through example as well as study in urban affairs. And while our college is surely not free from the pressure of the discipline of learning, the combination of a research-oriented institution with a small undergraduate college has given us the opportunity for many of the qualities sought—and frequently sought in vain—by the small liberal arts institution. But these results are in fact dependent upon the university's self-limiting goals; its recognition that its only uniqueness ultimately arises from the power of thought, the dedication to basic inquiry, the discipline of intellectual training. Even the university's role with other citizens and institutions in reestablishing its community—an emergency response, which might be thought to be an exception—would have been impossible without the recognition by the faculty who lived in the area that the continuation of the community was important because of the intellectual interdisciplinary values this proximity helped to support. That was basically why they wanted to live there. It would have been impossible also without the background of training, recognition of problems, and creativity which followed from the university's pio-

neering role of many years in the study of urban society. It is perhaps pardonable to say that a different
kind of university could not have saved the community. The university's role is not based upon a conception of neutrality or indifference to society's problems, but an approach to the problems through the
only strength which a university is entitled to assert.
It is a conservative role because it values cultures and
ideas, and reaffirms the basic commitment to reason.
It is revolutionary because of its compulsion to discover and to know. It is modest because it recognizes
that the difficulties are great and the standards demanding.

The assertion and existence of these values within
the university has given the institution a considerable
amount of freedom and a certain magic of wholeness.
One does not direct the University of Chicago to the
kinds of inquiry it should pursue, or the point of view
its professors should have. I assume there has been
no point of time when some professors' views were
not irritating to some segment of the community. In a
day when it is demanded by some groups that the
university as an institution take an official position
on social or political action, or close its campus to
those whose presence carries an unacceptable symbol,
this insistence upon freedom within the university
may appear either as outmoded or as a test of whether
the university really has meant what it has always
said. I think we have shown, and I trust we will show,
that we do mean this commitment to freedom—to
inquiry, to know and to speak. For those who regret
this conclusion, and believe a university can and
should be captured as an instrument for directed social change in the society, there is perhaps this com-

pensation: the world of learning is much too complicated to be directed in this way; the results would be
disappointing in any event. I cannot help but think,
although I am not sure the point is relevant, of the
casual businessman who feels sure that the teaching
of economics at Chicago has departed from classical
economic truth, and I place him alongside the casual-
trained economist who is sure there is something
wrong in Chicago's always having had the strongest
classical economics department in the country.

The freedom of the university and its scholars to
refuse to take on new assignments is extremely important. Universities today are involved in pressures
and temptations to respond to calls for all kinds of
social engineering and management tasks. Many of
these requests parallel similar demands for instant
medical cures and instant scientific discoveries. For
some of the tasks which the universities would be
given they are totally unprepared; neither professional skills nor scholarly disciplines have prepared
the way. Institutions which are in fact barely capable
of running themselves are now scrambling for the opportunity to tell others what to do. I recall a foundation official who some years ago thought it would be
a good idea if schools of education played a greater
part in running universities. He was not referring to
Chicago's eminent school. But his point was that
some schools of education called upon to advise foreign universities after World War II revealed they
were totally incompetent. For some reason this made
him think they should practice on their own institutions. Schools of education now have many demands
placed upon them, and this is true of many other areas
of the social sciences. The faculties at Chicago have

been selective and careful about accepting these assignments. The result is they have been able to concentrate on research and demonstration projects of far-reaching significance. It is no service to claim there is research where there is none; to assert special skill when none has been acquired. What is at stake is not only the character of American universities, but the very quality of American life. What is at stake also is our ability to develop the knowledge and skills to provide the answers which are sought. These must not be pretend answers.

I have referred to the sense of wholeness and a certain quality of magic. I recall the late Leo Szilard, puckish great scientist, describing the uncertain quality which made for a great laboratory. He could tell, he said, all the danger signals that indicated when things were not going well. But he could not say what made for a good or great laboratory. He only knew, he said, there was a sense of wholeness when this occurred. It was, he said in the most matter of fact way, a kind of magic. The University of Chicago in all probability could not be created today. The task would be too great and beyond reach. But the university can be refounded and recreated, as is the necessity for all institutions if they are to endure. The challenge to the university and its friends is to carry forward for our time this extraordinary tradition and instrument, which began all at once, assumed a unique combination of research, teaching, and professional training, and over its history has departed very little from the values it seeks. Perhaps this is why it carries also that magical sense of wholeness.

2

The Responsibilities of the Educated

Convocation address, University of Iowa
7 June 1968

For institutions and for men and women it is necessary to take counsel with ourselves, to rediscover values which lead us, to know again our own character and integrity. We are not deceived by promise for the future which none can know. We are not misled by formal achievement. We have a problem to solve, a life to lead. The problem is ourselves, our aims, our responsibilities.

The world is alarming. There is a war on—inadequately described as destructive, undeclared, and unpopular. It would indicate a dullness of soul or a false tact not to think of this agony, near to all, much nearer to many. There is renewed recognition of grave inadequacies in the openness of our society, in basic education, in social welfare, in the inclusion of minority groups within the economic order, in the control of violence and the acceptance of the ways of justice. The resulting crisis should be described in terms of these inadequacies, even though it appears in the form of social disorder with irrational and tragic consequences. We have "promises to keep" and "miles to go."

To some, the present perils have made our universities appear foolishly irrelevant. They are faulted for not taking a stand on Viet Nam, and for not having mounted a mass intellectual attack upon our social problems. Thus they stand accused of a lack of moral courage or virtue and a lack of organized brainpower or social commitment. Most universities and colleges would vote in hearty and overwhelming favor for the national position, whatever it is, in most wars. The lines of discussion would be closed, overwhelmed by moral patriotic fervor, catching and unquestioned. It is not very difficult to arouse this kind of moral fervor. When it occurs, universities are apt to proudly lose their uniqueness in the transcendent national emergency and to become great joiners. The present conflict is almost unique because it represents an attempt to conduct an undeclared war without the passion which would arise from a more customary total involvement. The absence of that much conforming passion, although people do feel passionately both ways, and the absence of customary wartime repression have permitted a continuing discussion of the wisdom of the national course. National policy has been under constant criticism and debate in the universities. The universities in this way have in fact continued to fulfill their function. Unfortunately the record is blemished. But these blemishes show how difficult free speech is. The blemishes argue against the declaration of institutional positions, which would find reality only in the further closing off of inquiry and debate.

The accusation that universities have failed to mount a mass intellectual attack upon social problems is a more interesting one. It frequently rides upon the analogy that if scientists could create an atomic bomb or eliminate through vaccine certain diseases, then they or others should be able to eliminate the causes of poverty, crime, or injustice. This Promethean concept is both basically anti-intellectual and too trusting of the instant wonders of the group mind. Discovery is the individual mind. There are not many minds capable of great advances. In this moment if we seek our truth we must admit how little we know, how shallow and overreaching our pretensions are. We can attempt to provide the environment for basic discovery. Through declarations, legislation, or whatnot, we can summon the spirits of the vasty deep. They do not come because we call them. Yet we should welcome this prod of impatience. There are areas where concern and service can be made more effective within the limits of present knowledge; where insights are only lost in the complexity of trivial research; where example and doing are good in themselves and a kind of discovery. So the impatience has relevance to the work of the universities. Basically, however, it is a call for social action, meaning by that a citizen's enlightened response to the problems of his day. That responsibility is upon each of us. It is difficult to discharge.

We would like our world to be unique. In most ways it isn't. To paraphrase, this is the best and worst of times, the age of wisdom, foolishness, belief, incredulity, light, darkness, hope, despair. We have everything before us; we have nothing before us; we are all going direct to heaven; we are all going the other way. Yet there are differences, if only, as Dickens suggested, in superlatives. For us, size is one difference. There are more of us and we tend to be crowded together. The size of the multitude—and we are of the multitude—makes even more important the fabric of trust and the rules for proceeding. But this trust and these rules are weakened by the movement of aspirations and the strange rhythm of life in an opening society. Then, too, we live under the domination of much more powerful and different means of communication. We have not mastered our responses to these new messengers. They convey, but they also substitute for reality. The sights and sounds which were always there confuse us, and, in truth, some never before existed. The result is the cliché; the slogan, the half-truth become sovereign through ritualized usage as we search for guides. The social sciences, founded in part to undermine the thoughtless stereotypes of an older age, have resolutely responded by creating new stereotypes. "It was many years before I learned the futility of engaging in controversy with the champion of the current vogues," a leading social scientist has written in his memoirs. But the powerful instruments of persuasion available today make this even more difficult. It is somewhat but not entirely unfair to say of the humanities that, deprived of their organizing view of knowledge and values, they have contributed to the confusion by their bitter remembrance of their old-time religion, their avid acceptance of what is frequently only the needlework of research, and by their mistaken envy of disciplines which seem to have relevance. In this atmosphere, commitment makes its own rules. Words are treated as weapons to be used if they work. At the same time, ambiguities of nonverbal communication are exploited. The end is taken to justify the means. But this has always been the way of faith over reason. Yet we need both.

The dangers to our inner life are many. One danger is simply that both faith and reason in any vital sense depart. Left to their own, they disappear. We have received much. It is not clear what we can make of what we have received. The time comes when our capacity for renewal is tested. Faith too easily becomes complacency; it must be replenished and rewon. Reason withers through disuse. So Howard Nemerov, in the mocking style of our time, celebrates the full professor who began his career with "some love of letters" and has survived, fattened on dissertations and as "a dangerous committeeman."

> Publish or perish! What a dreadful chance;
> It troubled him through all his early days.
> But now he has the system beat both ways;
> He publishes and perishes at once.

An equal, perhaps greater, danger is that we remain captive to the past. Can our faith, disciplined and then directed by reason, be strong enough to block not only the repetition and rhythm of our time, but the dreadful reaction to events long since gone? Violence has created violence. Evil has found its counterpart. The victim has copied the aggressor, and boredom has sought the excitement of prior pain. Even the ideas we hold are part of this pattern. Many of them have been tested and failed. We would know this if we took the trouble to find out what they mean and to see their consequences. Yet they persist, sometimes in different words but essentially the same. In this sense there is no generation gap—would that there were— but the reliving and reaction to prior woes and dreams. What mystery is this which causes us not to want to escape, but to confirm this automaticity, disowning personal responsibility, seeking success by embracing a false inevitability for the future? The partially educated are of course a menace, and we are all partially educated. The only practical remedy is to try to be more; to know the cultures which made us and others what we are; to know the history which warns of the ease and attractiveness of catastrophe and yet should be the base from which we can begin; to know the institutions which reflect our history and culture and yet can respond to the needs of our time; to know ourselves, for we must be the makers of choices, the judges of values. We seek a continuing liberation. But it is really not just a liberation of self which is sought but a shared understanding requiring a community of reason.

I trust we share a responsibility to make available to others the education we have received. The goal of universal basic education has not been realized. The opportunities have not been equal, and even if equal, they have been insufficient. Universities are an extraordinary heritage. They are among the most significant accomplishments in American history. Their origin has been varied—in church schools, liberal arts colleges, professional training, graduate institutes, or broadly based public education. Their sources of support over time have been very different. The demands made upon them, the specific objectives for service and training which have been set before them, have not been the same for all. The models which they copied were not the same and were put together in different ways. Yet out of this enormous range a new type of institution was created, unmistakably different from all that had gone before, an institution reflecting the energy of a new land, and so confident, that its enthusiasm saw few limits to the subjects to be taught, the proper fields of inquiry, the professions, vocations, or trades to be trained, the services to be rendered. One can decry the burden and folly of some of this exuberant indiscriminateness. Particularly now as more duties are urged each day, a university must order its purposes and measure its strength. But it is more important to emphasize the compelling concept, the transforming faith which moves communities to support and to continue to support—and scholars to organize and then give life to—the new academies. The compelling concept was a belief in the power of the free and yet disciplined mind as man's highest reach. This conception of freedom was and is startling and uncompromising. No wonder every university worthy of the name at one time or another over the years has had to resist attempts to control its teaching or inquiry. But a university used as a political instrument from without or within to that extent has simply ceased to exist. We should deny this power to ourselves and to others even as we welcome and underscore the concerns of political action as a personal duty of the educated citizen. This must be in our minds as we now take counsel.

The moment of reflection passes. Each of us will go his way. Yet we now are of a community—in some ways boundless and timeless; in other ways very much of the present. These responsibilities have waited upon us. They arise out of what we are. They give recognition to the membership we have won, to the powers we have sought to perfect, to the world which must be changed.

3

The Choices
for a University

A talk given on the occasion of Eugene Swearingen's inauguration
as president of the University of Tulsa
10 November 1967

A university, it has often been said, is a community. It is a community which is concerned with the individual—the individual scholar, the individual student. And these individuals of necessity are concerned with themselves. The student is going through a process which is intended to change him and to perfect his intellectual powers. It is a time of testing and emotional growth. The greater the education, the more disruptive the experience may be. The burden which each student carries is personal. The education which he seeks cannot be given to him; he must reach for it with himself. And though he seeks stars to steer by, he cannot escape the self-involvement which is essential if the process of education is to take place. The scholar is not so different. The contribution which he can make to his students and to the world of learning is of himself. It is not external to him. Intellectual powers wither through disuse, and are misguided or ineffective without the agonizing search for perfection which is the mark of the craftsman. The university community finds its fulfillment only through the work of the individual scholar and the individual student; and self-concern, which is not self-indulgence, is an essential ingredient.

But the university is something more than the work of individual scholars and students. Its own dimensions can be larger or smaller than the aggregation of individuals or component parts. It all depends on what kind of a university it is. It is not only that a university reaches in length of time beyond the span of any man, and thus represents the collective work of many generations; in addition, the university can add or subtract from individual efforts. By the direction it sets, the tone it creates, it can establish an environment which demands the best. It can establish an intellectual community in which individual efforts not otherwise possible will naturally flourish. By the pursuit of inappropriate goals, it can create an atmosphere which diminishes the efforts of all. The self-governance of universities denies the validity of the claim sometimes made that the individual scholar's loyalty should be only to his discipline and not to the institution. This is perhaps a luxury available to some, but it is a stolen luxury and no man's right. The individual self-concern of the scholar or student is not enough. There must be a general concern for the direction and values of the institution as a whole.

The examination of values and problems is required because all universities are forced to choices. The university which pretends to be all good things to all people is on the road to mediocrity. The university must decide what kind of a community it wishes to be. It is not enough to say that it is an academic community or a community of scholars. The university is one community among many; its members are members of other communities. What is to be regarded specifically in either a primary or a secondary sense as the business of the university? And what activities are to be placed in a subordinate role? Today universities have many opportunities and temptations, as, for example, to engage in many forms of research, both basic and developmental, to broaden the teaching to include many professional and vocational areas, to have international programs, and to assist cities in the development of cultural and artistic programs. The university must see itself within its own constituency and determine what its own road of integrity and quality is to be. This is not a message of resistance to change; quite the contrary. It is a plea that universities know what they are doing, judge their strengths and responsibilities, and then decide where they ought to go. Not all universities should be alike. American higher education draws great strength from diversity among institutions reflecting the many tasks to be done. The individual institution, like the individual scholar, repeatedly must go through the traumatic process of self-criticism, evaluating its own resources and possibilities, and setting new directions.

Self-criticism is made more palatable when it involves criticism of others. This is a day when slogans and beliefs concerning education have gained acceptance through repetition. These slogans are part of the popular culture which threatens to preempt all thought, and particularly all thought about education, even in the universities. In setting new directions it helps to penetrate below the surface of the popular sayings, even though this is only the first step in self-evaluation.

One such popular doctrine is the pursuit of excellence. This is the appropriate goal, the right one for this occasion. It sums up the choice of priorities which must be made. Yet it is correct to warn that the very concept can become a tranquilizer. There are many standards of excellence. If the standard is just short of perfection, it cannot be reached by very many. Perhaps for this reason, but certainly because of the egalitarian thrust of our society, excellence is now often thought to be tailor-made for each institution and each individual. Since, unfortunately, in many fields what a particular institution or individual can do is, at best, mediocre, what emerges is the strange conception of the excellence of mediocrity. It is an enormous and pleasing error to suggest that this transformation supports democratic values. It does not. Instead, it limits the most exciting possibility of a democratic society—the emergence of a changing aristocracy of ability. The road to achievement is surely long for all, but the remedy is hardly to destroy the road. This then is a plea, since goals can be assigned values which deaden thought, that the excellence which we seek be not determined by our abilities, but by the highest achievement available to man.

Another popular doctrine relates to the importance of the humanities as a course of learning which broadens the soul, removes the divisiveness of specialization, and helps to induce that civility which is important for an advanced democratic society. The conception is very odd. There is a good deal of history against it. Florence at the height of its culture was once described as a city torn by factions because it had so many humanists in it. There is much to suggest that the study of the humanities, in some cases, can induce a narrowness of spirit, and no field of learning is in fact less a field and more specialized. So far as civility is concerned, neither the modern novel nor the theater of the absurd suggests much of a contribution. Indeed, since the study of the humanities shares with other fields of learning the circumstance that it feeds upon itself—producing the books and training the teachers who comment upon the books—with the added advantage or difficulty that its subject matter consists of works of the mind, its view of the world always runs the danger of being strangely unbalanced. This is not intended in any sense as an attack upon the humanities, which would be a foolish position in the extreme, but rather as an indication of the problems to be met if the study of it is to achieve the goals which are sometimes claimed. Perhaps it depends upon how the humanities are taught.

There is another belief that man's understanding of himself and society has been vastly increased and is widely shared because of the growth of the social sciences. It is even believed that if the advice of social scientists were followed, many of our problems, domestic and foreign, would disappear or at least be mitigated. I suppose this is in a sense true. But there is another side. The growth of the teaching of the social sciences has been accompanied in some areas by the disappearance of historical knowledge. And the social sciences, like the humanities, tend to be highly specialized. Some of the areas tend also to be without much form. To a preoccupation with the strategies for minor investigation and an almost cynical fascination with the techniques for persuasion, has been added an array of topical concepts made almost meaningless because they are no longer rooted in any structure of thought, and because they are applied to situations for which they are inappropriate. This is not to disparage in any way the difficult pursuit of knowledge in an area which may be more complicated than that dealt with by the natural sciences, but to emphasize the distance between popular thought and the peaks of genuine contributions. Of course, techniques of investigation have been importantly used, advances in knowledge have been made. And the process of rediscovery for our time requires groping for ideas. Much of what appears as a criticism of the social sciences is rather a criticism of the condition of general education. Yet, it is a necessary accuracy to stress the unpreparedness of much of the social sciences, if it is to be treated as a profession, to point the way. The Pied Piper of Hamelin reappears in many forms. Some of the most egregious errors in planning have had the enthusiastic leadership of the purveyors of popular social science. And yet the problems of our society, such as the problem of mass education, which we are unequipped to solve, must be solved.

In the popular lexicon of higher education it is commonplace to denigrate professional schools as merely vocational. This indicates a misconception of the proper role of the professional school. It probably also indicates a misconception of the place for the purely vocational school. The downgrading of vocational schools is again a mistaken response to democratic values which, in fact, would be supported through the growth of some vocational schools. We ought not pretend they are something else. But the character of a professional school must be quite different. The professional school which sets its course by the current practice of the profession is, in an important sense, a failure. It cannot be this narrow and pedestrian and at the same time be effective. The professional school must be concerned in a basic way with the world of learning and the interaction between this world and the world of problems to be solved. This is true in medicine, in law, in engineering, and even in training for the ministry. It is true in other professions, including the profession of business, when it is viewed in this way. And because a profession is involved, a culture—a responsibility and an artistry—must be inculcated. It is not easy to create a new profession. This is indeed one of the problems of the social sciences. Viewed in terms of its larger responsibilities, the professional school inherits and exemplifies much of the disappearing tradition of the liberal arts college. As such it represents some of the highest values in a university. When a professional school does not exemplify these values, it suggests there is not only something basically wrong with it, but with the university of which it is a part, for the loss to both is great.

Practically everyone is in favor of liberal education. The enthusiasm is aided by uncertainty and confusion as to what it is. To some, it evokes a respite from the demands of the world—a soul-searching break between childhood and the demands of vocationalism to follow. To many, it is clear that whatever a liberal education is, it is not a professional education, although, as I have suggested, it may be that training for a profession is a liberal education. And, indeed, that is what a liberal education once was. To some, liberal education is general education, with the positive characteristic of including a variety of subjects, and the negative aspect of not concentrating too much on anything. But this overlooks the point that the very essence of education, no matter how it is approached, is the experience of working within and reworking a subject matter, and this requires concentration. The molders of public opinion are quite sure that liberal education requires teaching in contrast to research, which is regarded as dealing with facts and the knowledge machine and not with the ideas that count. But research properly conceived is the highest form of education. Without new insights and a new vision, no one can recreate for himself or for others the great traditions of the past, understand the cultures of today, or work with theory as a living structure. All of this is to suggest that there are a number of roads for liberal education. The popular guideposts are not much help. No road is easy, nor should it be, for we are talking about the perfection of the intellectual powers of the mind.

In a world of conflict and enormous problems, deluged with voices of mistrust, enchanted with popular doctrines and with the techniques of persuasion and coercion, the symbol and goal of the university has never been more important. The way of the university is the way of reason. Its faith is in the highest intellectual powers of man. Its commitment is to that discipline which characterizes the open mind, to the values which arise from the human endeavor, to the achievement of the self-criticism and honesty which is the morality of the highest intellectual integrity.

4

The University
and the Community

A talk given to the University of Chicago Club of Washington
Washington, D.C.
3 May 1968

41

I could use this occasion—and perhaps I am supposed to—to speak to you in what I hope would be an interesting way about the problems which the university faces. At least in less anxiety-ridden times, alumni who have retained or nurtured their affection for their university are reassured when the institution speaks of its worries. All institutions have problems. Awareness of them is some sign of life. Moreover, many problems can be translated into money. Alumni are always being asked for money. They usually respond generously. The pleasure is mutual. While it is bewildering to comprehend why so many new buildings are needed, alumni have a wonderful confidence that suitable aspirations will be realized. In the meantime, it is comforting to know that old Cobb Hall nearly fell down and was rebuilt with the old walls standing. Decay and rebuilding are reassuring signs of continuity, symbolizing the preservation of old values even in this age of need, affluence, and change. Your university is one of the great universities of the world. It is remarkable how much of it stands in its old form. It is constantly being rebuilt. But I hope I may be forgiven for not attempting to stir the coals of nostalgia at this time.

We do face many problems. We are overwhelmed by them. This is a time of enormous difficulty. Many of our concerns are echoes of conflict within the larger community. Education confronts the dilemma of a

society which believed in universal education but did
not provide it—a society which believed in openness,
but was closed for many. Customs and institutions
must now bend to help in the catching up process to
provide a new unity for action, a new acceptability
for goals. Most great universities throughout the
world are in cities; the cities are in trouble. The growing acceptance of forms of protest, including violence,
could in fact destroy the very idea of a university.
Currently, conscription for an unpopular war could
decimate the graduate schools. And there are special
financial concerns, arising out of the equation of ris-
ing living costs and increasing productivity for the
society as a whole. This equation could spell the
demise of many private institutions of higher learning—at least as private. So our problems range across
a broad spectrum, from our response to major responsibilities to the maintenance of our way of life, to
safety and security, and to financial complexities. But
these problems in turn force one to reexamine and restate the enduring purpose of a university—and if not
all universities at least this university—in our modern world. This central question of purpose, because
of the crisis of the larger world, presses most immediately upon the relationship between the university
and the community. Universities in many ways are
being asked, "What have you done for society
lately?" The question is sometimes made more biting
by the accusation that the conditions of modern life
arise out of the action or inaction of the universities
themselves. An easy although not always relevant example of this responsibility is the first self-sustaining
atomic pile on the campus of the University of Chi-

cago. Our society needs help. Universities are among our most important assets. What are they doing to help society solve its problems? The question is a troubling one and perhaps it is appropriate in this seat of political power, where the concerns are at least as great as they are elsewhere, to consider some of its implications.

Any history of the relationship between universities and their communities would have to recount the recent story of the University of Chicago. The university took the lead in a cooperative program to maintain and rebuild Hyde Park–Kenwood as a viable, integrated community. This was a result never before achieved in an American city. Pioneering creativity was required. New legislation, new forms of social organization came into being. Faith was required; not everyone had it. Important institutions fled the area, making a choice which the university had considered for itself but rejected. More than two hundred leading members of the faculty moved to other institutions in the fifties when it was not difficult to imagine the grass as greener elsewhere. One measure, but only one, of the effort involved is indicated by the financial side. The university itself spent thirty million dollars from its endowment for neighborhood purposes. This amount of endowment loss could spell the difference between a mediocre and a strong institution. As a consequence of the university's expenditures, an additional thirty million in funds and facilities came from federal and local government agencies. The private investment of one hundred and fifty million dollars followed as the program began to succeed. Other universities have been similarly involved in neighborhood redevelopment programs. But this is only one kind of community involvement.

The university's neighbor to the south is Woodlawn, where eighty thousand citizens live in a black ghetto community. On Sixty-third Street, in what was once a butcher shop, the university operates the Woodlawn Child Health Center as part of a program for the Chicago Board of Health. An advisory board of community leaders from Woodlawn helps to guide this clinic staffed by doctors and social workers. Within a six-month period this University of Chicago facility took care of 2,400 children from the area, with 6,300 individual visits, out of the 30,000 children in Woodlawn. In due time it is expected that this clinic will take care of at least 5,000 children. One block away, the university operates the Woodlawn Mental Health Center, led by university psychiatrists, with the guidance of a local Citizen's Advisory Board. This center has concentrated upon the needs of all of the first graders of the community, the 2,000 neighborhood children who yearly enter the school system for the first time. It is a program of assessment, guidance, and treatment, reaching into the twelve grade schools in Woodlawn and involving the parents as well as the children. Over a considerable period the university has worked with the Woodlawn Organization and with the School Board on a project to create an experimental school district in Woodlawn as a massive effort to create an educational system which will be more responsive and effective. It will involve elementary schools, an upper-grade center, and Hyde Park High School. The project, which at last seems to be reaching realization, will also involve the use of

school-community agents to establish a better relationship between the schools and the community, involving particularly the parents. On the university's
South Campus, the School of Social Service Administration is constructing a new Social Services Center to
coordinate existing social welfare agencies and programs of importance to the Woodlawn community.
The School of Education has embarked upon a program to train cadres of teachers for inner city schools,
directing the program to particular schools, involving
the training of new and present teachers—a program
of such emphasis and impact that, it is hoped, major
revisions within particular schools can be accomplished. But these are only some of the programs.
There are many more of which the following are only
a few examples: a neighborhood law office for the
poor, a student health organization to work in the
slums, an Upward Bound program for one hundred
students. There are eighteen separate programs for
Woodlawn alone. As you will have noticed, major
programs in a particular community have invariably
built upon community participation in the guidance
of the work. Governmental, foundation, and considerable university resources are involved.

I assume this presents a disturbing, yet perhaps
hopeful, picture. Disturbing because the needs are
enormous. Hopeful because immediate good may be
accomplished and understanding achieved for further
progress. These are serious service programs. The
University of Chicago's work with the community is
extensive at its best, unspectacular, and dedicated.
Research is involved, but one must not work with
people without primary concern for them. Service in
these programs is therefore primary. These activ-

ities impose a heavy cost upon the university and its
faculty. They require and reflect preferences and
choices—the allocation of precious resources of time
and energy. Moreover, they involve considerable administration and almost total involvement in day-to-
day practical affairs. Of course there are many other
programs relating to public policy at all levels in
which individual members of the faculties participate.

A prominent journalist and author, after inter-
viewing fifteen faculty members at a luncheon, and
being, I trust, duly impressed with them, expressed
his regret that Chicago was an ivory tower university,
concentrating on the theoretical rather than the practical. All faculty in the room agreed that Chicago's
role should be theoretical, basic, and long-term, rather
than immediate and practical. Unknown to the author, and perhaps to some of the faculty themselves,
was the fact that every member present in that room
was a member of one or more governmental task
forces or had recently been on a similar advisory
assignment. The theoretical university has responded
through its faculty to the challenge to attempt to
apply its knowledge to the practical order. It always
has. But what slide rule does one apply to judge the
suitability of extensive service projects within an institution said to be dedicated to the higher learning?
This question must be asked even though the need is
great and universities exist to serve society. These
statements in fact underline the importance of the
choice of service. Reference is sometimes made to the
precedent of the land grant colleges. The precedent
is quite ambiguous. The land revenues were to be
used for agricultural and mechanical education, yet
the greatest good came when these grants in fact con-

tributed to the strength of liberal and general education broadly conceived. Reference is sometimes made
also to the major funds now going to universities
from the federal government. But again these funds
either recognize, or are intended to increase, the
strength of the universities. And the question re-
mains: What strength and for what purpose? We
need guidelines, and it is natural that your university,
which has always been introspective and self-critical,
and which has always sought a central unity among
all its activities, should wonder about the relationship between this central unity and these new service
community functions. But there is another side to this
scrutiny of the place of service functions within a
university. This other side asks what the relationship is between these service functions and responsible government social action.

The service functions are enormously varied. While
research and education have a wide range, many of
these enterprises have little relationship to any special skill of the university. They range from running
a security force—the university spends twice as much
as does the city policing the Hyde Park–Kenwood
area—to urban redevelopment, with the mixed bag of
questions which that raises, to particular operations
such as clinics, where the university, initially at least,
clearly has something special to contribute. But there
is a long-term question even as to the special clinics.
Dr. Albert Dorfman, who is chairman of the Department of Pediatrics at Chicago and responsible for the
creation of the Woodlawn Child Health Center, has
commented that almost every medical school is planning or participating in some community health program. "The enthusiasm for such programs," he goes

on to say, "is based on novelty and naïveté. Eventually their weaknesses will appear no matter how enthusiastic their present reaction." He enumerates some of the weaknesses. "The portion of the population that can be served is only a tiny fraction of the need. The medical personnel available to medical schools is only a small fraction of the national pool. Almost all of the faculties of medical schools are chosen, quite properly, because of abilities as teachers and investigators. No medical school will survive if it requires highly skilled faculty to perform the routine tasks required for the performance of a successful community health program." Furthermore, "society is unlikely to finance such programs in the long term at levels of costs now being encountered." Dr. Dorfman justifies the present role of medical schools in community medicine as an attempt to "use their talent and inventiveness to examine the nature of the problem and discover solutions. Universities should not and cannot become administrative instruments of public or private services, but rather must be designers and innovators."

Undoubtedly a similar defense could be made of the University of Chicago's role in urban redevelopment. The university took the lead in collaboration with other community groups and with a responsive city administration. It drew upon the enormously talented yet varied ability within the university, including that of the chancellor and of the professor of urban studies. It had the advantage of a long tradition of the study of urban matters. An important result of that undertaking is to be found in the clearer vision and isolation of those urban problems which should not be dealt with on any long-term basis by universities as operating mechanisms. These are matters which must be worked out through the creation of new governmental structures within the network of local, state, and federal government, by a frontal attack on the unsolved problems of the relationships of cities and suburbs, by a much more determined and effective use of public facilities to establish proud communities. Our cities are in desperate need of replanning and rebuilding. The governmental problems far transcend any solutions which can be operated by a single private institution or group of institutions. There is something singularly sad about a New Deal or a Great Society which can only find the way and the means for an integrated society when there is a private institution available to give enormous funds before the government can respond, and even then is unable to respond in such a way as to build upon the natural assets of the community including the institutions within it. It is as though school systems, park systems, and police departments were to be had only on a matching basis. The cities cannot be saved in this way. There are simply not enough universities to go around for this purpose. And their powers quite properly are too limited in any event. A university is not a government. It is not good for the university, the community, or the government to think that it is.

The point then is quite simply that it is inappropriate for universities to be in charge of many of these services for more than an innovative and pioneering period—inappropriate because the universities are not the best means to carry through these programs effectively. Better means simply must be found. But you may think that some of my doubt is based upon a

fear of what the burden or opportunity of these programs will do to the universities. And to one university in particular. And you are correct. The proliferation of activities cannot help but place a strain
on the unity of the institution. When these activities
depart from the central purposes of the institution,
they inevitably involve a different kind of faculty or
staff. The question is not one of better or worse but
of the long-term effect on the entire institution. It is
all good and well to say that the institution should
change, but unless one means by this that its central
purposes should also be modified, this argument
raises the question of why this institution? Why
would it not be better to create new institutions for
these purposes? Of course I realize there are many
who do not believe that the central purposes of universities as they have been are very important. But I
do not agree with them. It is easy and natural for universities to claim too much, to forget their proper
aims, to speak with many tongues to gain support.
The results of overproliferation and expansion within
universities are there for all to see. They are not comforting. Commissioner of Education Howe frequently
talks about the responsibilities and failures of universities. In a recent speech, as quoted in the *New York
Times*, he has again alluded to the failure of the university, which, as he says, has the temerity to change
the world but "has not the nerve to adapt itself to the
world." The contributions listed as changing the
world have to do with being responsible for the reach
into space, for splitting the atom, and for "the interpretation of man's journey on earth." I had not realized that the universities had been able to supply
that much-needed interpretation, but one can accept

the point that universities are engaged in the pursuit of knowledge and that knowledge changes many things. So does ignorance. It is quite another thing—and indeed quite the opposite thing—to suggest that universities, like everyone else, must adapt to the world. A great deal of the strength of the university comes when it does not adapt to the world.

One has to ask again what is the greatest service of the university. Its greatest service is the preservation of an intellectual tradition. The university is the home of ideas. Many of these ideas are incorrect and foolish. Many are persuasive, dangerous, and devastatingly impractical. Faculties are not selected for a general ability to be prudent and practical. If the desire is to make of universities one more governmental agency, then of course all that will result is one more governmental agency. The vision of the university does not come from Health, Education, and Welfare. It does not come from the professional educationist. It comes from a tradition where knowledge is really sought for itself. And it is on this basis that universities are worth supporting, for therein lies their difference.

We live in a curious time. There never has been in the history of the world as much conversation broadcast on a widespread basis by the mass media reflecting the thoughts of almost everyone on almost every conceivable subject. That conversation reveals what every study of opinion has shown—that people have strange ideas, that commonplace views are really not the glory of a civilization. They never have been. This is one reason we have a bill of rights and a constitution in order to force a sober second thought. There is an enormous job of education to do. And there is a task of leadership. But the continuing task of education and leadership requires, if the continuity of civilizations is to be maintained and understood, places of deliberate and structured thought. It requires the examination of problems of our time free from the necessity of appearing to be relevant or popular, or even, finally, correct. From this kind of pursuit will come the few ideas which will change the world. If universities, or at least a remaining few universities, cannot fulfill this function, then we had better create institutions of higher learning, free from the demands of mass culture and service, to perform this function.

I know this speaks against a popular wind. Let me make clear what I am not saying. I am not saying that controlled exposure to problems of the society cannot be important for education and for research. This exposure has given great strength to professional schools; but it is controlled exposure. There is a duty upon all institutions, including education, to do their part to unify the society in which we live and to help fulfill the openness of that society, including most particularly the paths of the intellect. But undue reliance upon universities as handy agencies to solve immediate problems remote from education can only end in the corruption of the universities. And the danger is greater because corruption is easy and attractive, particularly when it is dressed up as a relevant response to the problems of our day. The danger is greater, not because we should be against these activities, but on the contrary because we must be for many of them. The burden upon the universities is particularly heavy because they know they must relate to and indeed must help create those professions and other institutions in our society which will transmit and put into service the basic knowledge which flows from our institutions of higher learning. We must, for example, create networks of medical care, of adult educational enterprises, of new kinds of education for primary and secondary schools, and new channels for the social sciences, so that the ideas of the academy can be tested, rejected, corrected, and put into use. The universities must be related to these networks. But the risk is great that in doing so the universities will lose their protected remoteness, their freedom to be objective, their determination to seek intellectual truth on its own terms. This would be the greatest disservice. The problem is how to create these networks and, in part, to create them for the very purpose of preserving the inner strength of the universities.

What then are the guidelines? I have done little here except to stir the questions. Surely among the guidelines is a continuing awareness that universities are not governmental agencies; that universities do not speak for communities, but that communities must speak for themselves; that university service operations must not become so routinized and habitual that they are continued in this way when others could do them just as well or better. Beyond this, a university must know its own character. It is not enough to say it is dedicated to education and to the cultivation of intellectual pursuits. It must be able to see itself as a whole in spite of diversity. To see itself as a whole requires a recognition throughout the entire enterprise of the primacy of the commitment to teach and thus preserve the cultures of many civilizations— of the primacy of the commitment to basic inquiry and to the candor and discipline of reason. Perhaps the answer is that the limits of the institution's growth must be compatible with these commitments. The continuing strength and unity within will measure that growth. Perhaps all this means is that one must work harder to build up the central strength if there is to be growth at the periphery.

We can, I hope, be proud of the contributions which the university is making to service in the community. I hope also that we are strong enough and confident enough of our ability to preserve our central purpose to continue these commitments, to be a good neighbor and not the great house on the hill, to help our troubled society return to health, and to preserve that proper power which is the power of the reasoned word.

5

The University,
the Professions,
and the Law

A talk given on the occasion of the dedication of the
Earl Warren Legal Center, University of California at Berkeley
2 January 1968

This new legal center proudly carries the name of the Chief Justice of the United States—a name synonymous with the law's responsiveness and concern. The Earl Warren Legal Center is a commitment to professional social action. Ours is a society in transition. Our aspirations are high. Our pride has been great. Knowledge and control over nature have increased. The society, or at least a considerable portion of it, is affluent. But these factors make less acceptable our present situation. Urban squalor and crime, the contamination of the environment, our failures in education, the inequality of citizenship for the poor, the consequences of continuing war—all these press upon the conscience of the community. For the quality of life in a society in transition, the role of law is pivotal. The law's procedures, providing means for participation and fulfillment of the sense of fairness, can draw the society together and give stability in change. Moreover, the operation of the legal system causes or retards change. The craftsmanship of the law is tested by its ability to respond to, and in a sense create, felt needs. This new law center expresses a confidence in the relevance of the work which can be accomplished here, both for the quality of life in our present society and for the movement toward the realization of those persuasive, albeit changing, goals which we have set for ourselves.

It is characteristic of the comradeship of the bar

that the center should be placed within a complex which makes available rooms for residence and with facilities to be used by judges, lawyers, law professors, and law students. Custom, cohesiveness, and collective responsibility are of enormous importance to our calling. Perhaps this is why the Inns of Court remain as a romantic ideal for the American lawyer even though centuries ago the rise of easy printing disrupted the enforced comradeship among lawyers and law students, and made less important the relationship of judges as teachers with the students' box in the courtroom. The ancient college, established as a residence unit in part to keep "the undisciplined swarm of rowdy, irresponsible and other dissolute boys and youths from fourteen upwards" off the streets where their "riots and misdeeds" were a public nuisance, in the modern age has become the basis of a special environment for law students within the larger university. Now the law center, through seminars, work shops, continuing education for judges and lawyers, law revision and research, at least symbolically—and perhaps with more reality than that—extends this environment to the profession as a whole.

It is characteristic of our age that the law center, an institution intended to conduct and translate research into service and action, should be located within a university. There are today insistent voices stressing the service duties of universities. One such strong voice is that of the Secretary of Health, Education, and Welfare, John Gardner. The secretary points to the enormous problems to be solved. He writes: "We can build gleaming spires in the heart of our cities, but we can't redeem the ghettos. We can keep people alive twenty-five years beyond retirement, but we can't assure them they can live those years in dignity. We choke in the air that we ourselves polluted. We live in fear of a thermonuclear climax for which we provided the ingredients."

The secretary is not too complimentary about what universities have accomplished. "Consider," he says, "our most grievous domestic problems—the cluster of interlocking problems centering around poverty, the cities, and the Negro. One would like to think that the universities have been the primary source of intellectual stimulation and enlightenment on these issues. One would like to think that university research on these matters had laid the basis for significant action." "Unfortunately," he comments, "this is far from the truth. There are brilliant and effective members of the academic world who have contributed to our approach to these problems. But generally speaking . . . one cannot say the universities are a significant intellectual base for the main attack. In fact, a good many university people . . . barely understand what the relevant problems are. Many are debating policy alternatives left behind five years ago."

The secretary then calls upon the universities to manifest "a focussed, systematic, responsible, even aggressive concern for the manner in which the society is evolving. . . ." "We need," he writes, "to be told how to build a better society, and how to get from here to there. Most of all, we need help in the difficult business of changing institutions. Those parts of the university which are already involved in extensive interaction with the larger community are going to have to take the responsibilities of that relationship more seriously than ever before."

There are quite a few professors who might be willing to tell the secretary how to build a better society. Their advice might not be always usable. The chairman of the English Department in a technological university has recently bitterly denounced the misuse of the study of literature. Instead of seeing an increasing number of students and courses in this area as a response to the opportunities of the leisure society, he ascribes this growth to the necessity of capitalism to expand to avoid collapse. In his view, the university's institutional function is to contribute to the technological triumphs of capitalism, and departments of literature are as deeply involved in this as departments of industrial management. "The more Viet Nams," the professor writes, "the more endowed chairs." Instead of viewing the study of an art form as an inquiry into models of excellence, he adopts the view that the study of literature should be an instrument of social change, beginning with an examination of social needs. Literature should be used as a form of agitation to undermine the status quo, to touch the raw nerve, "to remind students of human possibilities, of the reality of feelings, of both horror and beauty," even though this won't "stop the butchery in Viet Nam."

Some might call the critic a dissenter. Secretary Gardner recognizes that he would "not wish to see anything happen that would alter the character of the university as a haven for dissent and for creative scholarly work." So the statement of the discussion of the trustees of the Carnegie Foundation for the Advancement of Teaching concludes that public service is one of the three functions of the modern university, but cautions that public service also means sanctuary for the dissenter. The caution is appropriate. An institutional approach to the solution of problems would restrict the freedom of the individual scholar. Even without an institutional approach, too close a connection between thought and action might also inhibit. The resignation of the Quakers from the government of the colony of Pennsylvania when there was a war to be fought with the Indians was probably good for both the Quakers and the colony. But it is not the function of a university to govern, and a university needs dissenters because ideas are important. An implication that dissenters in our society can find their only sanctuary within a university ought to be —and I think is—an unfair description of our society. It is similar to the view that the universities must support the performing and creative arts because no one else is interested.

When Secretary Gardner asks for a more intentional direction of effort toward solving the problems of society, he is asking for professional work. Professional work carries its own responsibilities. The scholar's concern and even his complete personal involvement is not sufficient to create a profession. Contrary to the modern view, there was a time when universities were much more professional than they are now. The medieval university directed its work toward the needs of the three major professions of theology, law, and medicine. These callings exercised sovereignty over large realms of knowledge and action. Knowledge was viewed as both unified and purposefully related to a discipline with responsibility for its application. There was less specialization but also less freedom. It is not at all clear that the literary critic's view of international relations, philosophy, and economics would have been considered appropriate within that framework. Today, with the growth of specialization and freedom, we ask of the individual scholar only that he formulate his views so that they may enter into some kind of a marketplace for rational discussion. And sometimes the scholar does this. It is assumed the exchange of ideas will build upon the individual work of many persons, and we rely on this process to somehow achieve a kind of coherence. Furthermore, there is no one profession for the social sciences—no profession which monitors and brings together knowledge and experience to answer grievous domestic problems. Perhaps the universities have not been the significant base for an intellectual attack upon many of these problems. But there has been no effective substitute for the universities either.

A learned government consultant, an expert on universities, has cataloged the assets the university can contribute toward building the Great Society. These are staff, buildings and grounds, a climate within and prestige without, objectivity, a commitment to search for new knowledge, and the fact that universities have values and stand for something. He includes human talent, but remarks there is substantial evidence that neither the government nor the universities hold their share of superior intellects. This is because the rewards of the profit-making world are so much greater. This catalog, while correct, is harrowing. Objectivity, the commitment to values, and the search for new knowledge can be lost or distorted if the university is misused. The climate within can be ephemeral. Staff, buildings, grounds, and prestige do not make a university. The suggestion that lesser talent must be sufficient because the better minds are in commercial fields either demeans the complexity of the problems to be solved, or suggests the universities cannot be the best place to solve them. The essential power of a university is the power of the individual mind, disciplined by the requirement that ideas be objectively stated and reexamined. The objectivity required is analogous to what is meant by the rule of law and not of men. Just as the rule of law summarizes a relationship among institutions and men which protects freedom, so the rule of ideas is essential to the accomplishment of the modern university. The idea must be objectively stated so that it is free from its originator, can be translated and reexamined in the light of other disciplines and many cultures, and can meet the tests and the corrective process imposed by the forces of other ideas. This is the rational process. It is sometimes attacked because the unconscious, the emotional, the concern for human values, and the need for action are thought to compete with or to override the rational approach. These are also sometimes suggested as tempting reasons for by-passing the rule of law. But the nature of the subject matter to be examined, the agony or accident of discovery, the intentions or commitment of the individual scholar do not substitute for the rethought objective statement. Yet all would agree that somehow ideas must be made more relevant to present problems.

This is the function of the professional school and of the professions. It is through the professions that ideas developed and discussed within universities find their way to treatment and application. It is through the professions that a better conception of problems to be met is brought to the universities for analysis. The relationship is intricate and continuing. The profession itself is involved in the creative process. It develops institutions of its own to facilitate the bringing together of ideas and problems. It has its own customs, its own sense of group responsibility and purpose. It develops the craftsmanship necessary for understanding and application—a craftsmanship which itself reflects a group judgment as to what the main problems are. It is concerned with the continuing education of its members and the training of successors. The professional schools within universities reflect this concern; at the same time they represent the profession in the examination of basic problems and relevant ideas. The prototype of the overall relationship can be seen in the field of medicine, where the physician, the institutes, the hospitals, the medical schools, and the universities form an interrelated complex. When the system operates properly—and this is a problem for any profession—the exchange of ideas as to problems and theories is continuous. The physician, whether or not he is on a medical school faculty, or in a university hospital, or in a group clinic, or in practice by himself, has a relationship to the continuing research of the universities and institutes. And the profession provides group action for the solution of problems—that, after all, is what a hospital is.

I realize that in using this example of medicine at a law gathering, I have done worse than bring coals to Newcastle. The error in prototype is that it doesn't quite apply outside its field. Moreover medicine, while a favorite analogy used by legal educators— think of the phrase "legal clinics"—has its problems of organization. The social ailments with which law must deal have their own difficulties, although both law and medicine are confronted with contagion and group problems, and both are concerned with conditions closely related to the structure and operations of our society, in which individual effort by the most dedicated professional may seem ineffective. In any case, I have idealized both the universities and the professions. The relationship between them is frequently not that close or rewarding. Arrangements may look fine on the surface but there is not much underneath. The professions like to be masters in their own house. They determine what the house is. The scope of a profession is determined by the institutions it serves, custom, and theoretical structure. Of course, no profession can know everything. It must delimit its boundaries. Yet in doing so it may fail to examine the very problems which should be at the focus of its attention. If the poor have no legal problems, or at least no problems interesting to law students, perhaps this should be a major concern for the law schools and the profession.

There is a natural lag in the perception of problems. The fragmentation of knowledge has increased this tendency. This fragmentation is matched by the proliferation of professions or quasi professions. There is competition among advice givers. Remedies which are proposed are likely to reflect the particular bias of a segmented discipline, and often without the process of consultation and growth which a profession ought to give. Perhaps all of this is grist for what is called the decision-making process in a democratic society. But it removes the thoughtful, coordinating influence of a profession at the point where it is most needed. All of this is to say, again, there is no one profession for the social sciences. To reuse the medical analogy, if there is to be no first, general, or coordinating physician in the modern world, then some kind of new institutional arrangements will have to develop to replace him.

But the lawyer, even though the bar also reflects the growth of specialization, has always prided himself on being a generalist. His discipline touches most aspects of men in society. He deals in persuasion and therefore is required to believe in the liberal arts, which are a generalizing influence. James Madison advised a young friend to study law because, Madison said, "it alone can bring into use many parts of knowledge you have acquired and will still have a taste for, and pay you for cultivating the arts of eloquence. This cannot be said so truly of commerce and physics and therefore less learning and smaller understanding will do for them." I regret to say Madison adds, while commending his friend's determined adherence to probity and truth in the character of a lawyer, that he fears "that would be impracticable." But that was because there might be "misrepresentation from a client or intricacy in a cause."

The profession honors, in tradition at least, the connection between the discipline of law and other sciences which relate to human nature. The case method has chased out of the modern law school most of the lectures on moral philosophy which once adorned the university study of law. But the discussion of cases themselves is in the liberal arts tradition of the examination of men, motives, and sometimes consequences. And the lawyer sees himself as a co-ordinating influence, a strategic intermediary between people, between the government and the individual, between ideas and their application. Listen to Karl Llewellyn's description: "The essence of our craftsmanship lies in skills, and in wisdoms; in practical, effective, persuasive, inventive skills for getting things done, any kind of things in any field; in wisdom and judgment in selecting the things to get done; in skills for moving men into desired action, any kind of man, in any field; and then in skills for regularizing the results, for building into controlled, large-scale action such doing of things and such moving of men. . . . We concentrate on the areas of conflict, tension, friction, trouble, doubt—and in those areas we have the skills for working out results."

The Earl Warren Legal Center, I would suggest, will find its greatest opportunity for service if it takes seriously the ability of the lawyer as generalist and as a coordinating influence. This occasion cannot help but emphasize the central task of law in perfecting basic values. The questions to be answered are the perennial great ones. Witness the resurgence in our time of natural law questions: If the ordinance which is contrary to higher authority need not be obeyed, why should the law which is contrary to higher ideals be enforceable? What is the place within our own society for civil disobedience? The Supreme Court indeed in our own times has had to determine a question of massive civil disobedience. In the history of our country the record of the Supreme Court of the United States under the leadership of Chief Justice Warren is unparalleled in the effective attention given to the development of constitutional doctrines to safeguard the dignity of the individual. The accomplishment is awesome. It ranges from the basic rights of

accused defendants, to the reapportionment of legislatures, to the protection of free speech, assembly,
teaching, and association, to freedom of conscience,
to the right to equal education. And any lawyer could
add to this list. The court has thus been concerned
with the wellsprings of our society. But I am sure
the chief justice would agree that many of the decisions point directions for work which cannot be accomplished by the court by itself. New tasks have
been presented for the bar and for public and private
agencies; new responsibilities have been imposed
upon the individual citizen.

The court system is indeed the guardian of basic
rights, which are the law's special concern. But I trust
the Earl Warren Legal Center will not have as its emphasis the study of the work of the Supreme Court
of the United States or the Supreme Court of California. I understand that in the work of these and
other courts there is much to study, and much to in-
terpret and clarify. But this is what the law schools
have been doing for years. No doubt they will continue to do so. But as the career of the chief justice
himself shows, there are other law agencies, and there
is the bar itself.

The separation which we see today between court
and legislature should not hide the fact that the obligation for perfecting law is at least as much on the
legislatures, and some would say more, as it is upon
the courts. And lawyers who are members of legislatures should hardly be thought on that account to
have removed themselves from the tasks of the profession. It is of course true that the courts have possession of the wand, goad, or hammer of constitution-
alism. I do not join some of the critics of the courts,

who review cases and opinions as though they were plays, in deprecating the growth of constitutional doctrine. But this does not prevent the expression of sorrow, which all members of the bar should feel, that so many steps which should have been taken because they are wise were only taken, and if then, when the courts made them necessary. Moreover, it should be said that in many instances the constitutional decision cannot by itself settle the larger problem, and the true effectiveness of decisions must wait until the other agencies of the bar and of society catch up.

The Earl Warren Legal Center has the opportunity to examine in depth some of the pressing social problems which mark a society in transition. I refer to Secretary Gardner's listing of those issues which weigh upon everyone. He mentions the cluster centering around poverty, the cities, and the Negro. Of course these are not just legal matters. But they do involve the law in many ways. They have a legal base, and we are supposed to be the generalists and coordinators. Think of some of the characteristics of our public school systems. The average current expenditure in 1965 for the east south-central states was $354 per pupil in the primary and secondary public schools. The comparable figure was $732 for the middle Atlantic states. Of course the cost of living varies, and there is no reason anyway to suppose that one dollar for education has the same value for all places. Nevertheless, the difference is rather great and does mark a national problem. These discrepancies also occur within a single state. They occur between suburbs surrounding a single city. For example, the expenditure per high school pupil in a suburb to the north of

Chicago is $1,283; in a suburb to the south of the city it is $723. The expenditure per elementary school pupil in a northern suburb is $919; in a southern suburb it is $421. Major differences occur between the suburbs and adjacent cities. And within cities. The students are compelled by law to go to school. It is state action which brings them there. It is state action also which has made the school districts. "Today education is perhaps the most important function of state and local governments. Compulsory school attendance laws and great expenditures for education both demonstrate our recognition of the importance of education to our democratic society. . . .[I]n these days, it is doubtful that any child may reasonably be expected to succeed in life if he is denied the opportunity of an education. . . ."* Is there any reason to believe that the opportunity for required education is really equal when there are these extraordinary differences—and the examples are many—which occur between suburbs of the same city within the same state? And is this discrimination in the operation of this most important function of state and local government to be justified because this is the way the ball bounces; that is, this is how the state action happens to collect and happens to allocate funds for the education it requires of all?

I have stated the questions in this form to suggest, as I believe, that there is a strong argument to be made for the unconstitutionality of certain aspects of the present system. But I would hope this and other legal centers would take problems of this kind in their larger dimension. Not only law is involved. Methods and systems of education, the governance of the sub-

* *Brown v. Board of Education* 347 U.S. 483 (1954).

urbs and adjoining areas, the tax systems which make for inequalities—all these and more have their impact. If coordination can be provided for these problems, concentration given and followed through, the relevant social sciences brought to bear, their interest awakened by the larger picture, then a magnificent contribution can be made. I am not speaking of a conference. I am speaking of that relationship between research and alternatives of thought-out action which can draw to itself the ideas to be found within the universities and from the concerned professions, of on-going work which will build upon itself, and will stay with the problems until solutions are reasonably worked out and made clear; and then explained, reviewed, and corrected through the instrumentalities of continuing education.

This is not a new call for research and action. It has been made to the law schools many times. The Earl Warren Legal Center should make possible that kind of thoughtful research and coordination which will make a difference. Perhaps this will be beyond the capability of the law centers. But this center is so nobly named, it should not fail in its mission.

6

General, Liberal, and Specialized Education

A talk given to the Association for General
and Liberal Education, Chicago
25 October 1963

If all activities with which the University of Chicago is charged are taken into account, the budget is in excess of $170,000,000.* The budget reflects the responsibilities of a university caught in the necessities of the modern world. There is a fierceness to the strains imposed upon the modern university as it attempts to keep itself a viable and effective community of scholars. A sense of fatigue is more likely to accompany budget making than are thoughts or ideas, bright or otherwise. I suppose at such times, among other occasions, there is an inevitable tendency to think back to the days when liberal education was simple or central—or at least we can pretend that it was—and to deplore the departure of the universities from the straight, albeit broad, path of liberal and general education. It is frequently popular to believe that universities have deserted liberal education, and to imagine that liberal education is to be found only in those liberal arts colleges which do not already conceive of themselves as universities and which exist affluently or precariously, but pleasantly, between up-graded high schools and research-driven institutions of higher learning. Such thoughts are pernicious —in part because they are wrong. Of course, I do not mean that the problems of either liberal or general education are simple in either the universities or, meaning no disrespect, in Old Siwash, beneath the

* As of October 1963.

elms. The problems are somewhat different in the two types of institutions even though there is a good deal of Siwash in all of us. Indeed it would not be surprising to find there was more of Old Siwash in the more complex institutions of higher learning than in the colleges. The difference may be important to us but the point is that there is a relationship between research and specialization, and liberal and general education. If the mixture causes problems, perhaps it also has advantages.

Because I may sound critical of certain tenets of liberal or general education, I should say at once that I admire the College of the University of Chicago. I believe that the College has made the intellectual tradition the challenging and question-inducing focus of campus life. It is not unique in that, of course, but it has been persistent and pioneering. It collected its thoughts on what education was about when it was popular to leave that to the students. It developed one of the first general-education courses, "The Nature of World and of Man," and when that caught on, changed its direction to cultivate the required broadly gauged group—taught courses in the basic disciplines and skills of the liberal arts. I would not say that all of this was done with the greatest modesty in the world, nor was the Message to the Gentiles always as pleasing or as persuasive as it might have been. But a certain amount of tension is good in education as elsewhere. The excitement among the faculty and, therefore, the students has been real. If at times the College has loved excitement more than winning ways, this reminds us that not even at Chicago can one have everything. And the influence has been widespread and good for American education. Surely, not many schools can point to such a record of contribution to collegiate life.

But I have some questions about general and liberal education which, even though they are not directed specifically at the College, are intended to apply there as well as elsewhere. In any event, perhaps it may be useful to express doubts concerning some widely and deeply held views.

Since I am an ex–law school dean, it is not surprising that I should have some doubts concerning the legitimacy of the fears of professionalism and specialization which seem endemic to liberal arts and general studies programs. Some of the fear is justified, of course, but I think this depends on the way professionalism and specialization are approached. In any event, it is a fact that law schools, perhaps erroneously, often think of themselves as giving a kind of liberal education at the graduate level. It is a program of great intensity, made more intense because there is a seriousness of purpose in part derived from an awareness that a craft is being learned and that craftsmanship makes a difference and must work. We did not believe that the fact that there was seriousness of purpose, and involvement in doing, rather than solely an appraisal of what was being done, detracted from the liberal arts training, nor did it occur to us that there was any particular handicap that the education was at the graduate level. All that I am saying, if I am correct, is that professionalism and specialization by themselves may not be incompatible with liberal arts education. The arts and techniques for law school work are reading, reasoning, and speaking, an ability to relate values and concepts in operational structures and to make judgments which involve justice in action as the result of the application of the general to the specific. These seem to be of the liberal arts, and while it is not strictly germane to my theme I think some recognition should be given to the part which professional schools play within universities, because they now represent a merger of the teaching and research traditions when this merger is so important and so much needed. Possibly I may be forgiven with this misshapen background if I wonder at the assumption sometimes made that the liberal arts and general studies are solely undergraduate matters, and that freedom from specialization in depth is perhaps not a desired but an inevitable element in a successful liberal arts and general studies program.

By now it is, of course, clear that I do not know what the liberal arts are, and I am not sure what is intended by general studies. Somehow there seems to be something unsatisfying about the roster of liberal arts if by that is meant grammar, logic, rhetoric, geometry, arithmetic, astronomy, music, and perhaps medicine and architecture. It is difficult to be against these items, but they do not seem to be the precise categories for identifying the skills and techniques necessary for intellectual and cultural life. The categories seem to be a matter of history and therefore of treasured learning, and they suggest, but I wonder if they identify, the ways of thought and the technical skills necessary for modern knowledge and intellectual creativity. In any event, I doubt if many would think these categories spell out a curriculum. I am not sure the matter is helped much by adding the concept of general studies, if by that is intended (and I realize there are other meanings) the exposure of the student, usually through the required grouping of courses, to the major ingredients in the major fields of knowledge characterized as humanities, social sciences, and the natural sciences, with some additional work perhaps in mathematics, history, and language. And all this to be accomplished primarily in the first two years of a college program. One can say of the liberal arts approach that it is of the essence of any intellectual education, for its concern is the working out of the theoretical framework which gives meaning to an unruly subject matter, the ability to work this framework, and to understand through the competition of other disciplines the relationships of compatibility or incompatibility arising out of the purposes for which these structures are used. But I am not sure that these lessons can be learned in what are essentially survey courses, even though the name is now anathema, and survey courses in subject matters which are not themselves organized—in some instances at least—with any unity of theory. The conflict between disciplines within the unorganized subject matters would be highly educational if there were time and opportunity to explore in depth. But a social science course which touches upon some economics, some psychology, some sociology, and some supreme court cases may turn out to be education in the liberal arts when it becomes an exercise in reading and rhetoric. But it does not have time to explore the structures in depth, and it can never know what the competition among the disciplines really is.

In short, I doubt whether the guided trip through the various subject matters can be accomplished in the spirit of the liberal arts. It is necessarily superficial, even though it may give training in reading, speaking, and writing of a limited kind. There is, therefore, perhaps a lack of seriousness, or a failure of craftsmanship, not in terms of the instructor but in effect, which should be devastating to any liberal arts conception. Moreover, I fail to see why the complete guided tour is necessary either from the standpoint of a roster of skills or techniques or in order to make of the student a decently balanced individual. The desire to educate the whole man, meaning by that many of the facets of growing up, was once greeted with great scorn on the Chicago campus in order to give emphasis instead to intellectual skills and the works of the mind. One may wonder at the necessity for the exclusion of the creative arts and other omissions which placed history and language in limbo. But it surely was not desired to replace the whole man with the evenly educated man—with the smattering well balanced, although of course worse things than that could happen to a student. All of us naturally, I think, tend to overemphasize formal instruction and the place of examinations in the educational process. A proper university or college would have many lectures, concerts, plays, and discussion groups. And interactions within the university community, if matters are properly attended to by the faculty, can fill many of the gaps which will save a student from the dreadful consequences of not having had a formal course covering the more superficial aspects of art, poetry, or the Supreme Court's view of segregation, to take some examples where I clearly mean no offense. What I am arguing for is exploration in depth and an appreciation of craftsmanship and of technical skills of all kinds, including the grubbiest, where mechanical contrivances are seen as extensions of works of the mind, with the responsibility of the professional felt deeply because the structure is not merely observed but is made to work. Of course, I am not saying that all survey or superficial approaches should be ruled out. But I doubt if they do much for the liberal arts, and I am pleading for some room for intensive study, which, if sufficiently pursued, will bring many subject matters together. I am aware that possibly I am urging a form of education which the red brick universities of England are deserting, but while these universities are no doubt very good and should be encouraged, I am not certain we must follow them.

I do not believe the specialization of craftsmanship is provided by the system of majors in the last two years of college work. Specialization requires its own unity and determined purpose. The bazaar of the first two years of college life, during which the departments in effect flash their wares at the students, is replaced by a cafeteria in which the student is allowed to pick and choose from a bewildering array of courses and programs, and where, although I am sure it frequently occurs, one cannot be sure that any community of scholars exists with which the student can identify and which identifies with him. I am not so much concerned about the freedom of the student to pick and choose, but his lack of opportunity to find the coherent and intensive programs which I suggest should be at the center of his education.

Just as I think it is impossible to organize all knowledge for the student in his first two years, unless the thrust is a philosophical program in depth, which has its own form of specialization, I also think it is important that the separate subject matter courses of the last two years form part of a coherent whole, which results from organizing a discipline in its main dimensions. There ought to be a faculty which feels a commitment to this organization and is concerned about the progress of the student in the field as a whole. And because there is a relevance in other disciplines, and because education is not merely specialization, such a faculty should feel a concern, too, to see to it that the exposure of the student to subjects and arts outside his main field continues at this higher level.

One theme which runs through what I have said is the relevance of research to teaching and learning. The structures of the intellectual world can be admired, but they are never truly known until they have been worked with, used to comprehend new knowledge, and refashioned to repair the damage done to them by new facts or theories not previously accounted for. There is a unity to knowledge to be sought after, and the community of scholars adds to the successful pursuit of research when it tries to explain the framework contemporaneously arrived at by the separate disciplines. This generalizing and explanatory function can be one of the great contributions of the liberal arts college to the research drive of a university. There should be a natural affinity, therefore, between the liberal arts and the research functions of the university. Possibly a better organization of undergraduate study would break down the barriers between undergraduate and graduate work not because the college is regarded as preparatory but because participation in research illuminates the field of study. And because the competition of many disciplines is wholesome and revealing in increasing measure as greater competence is achieved, it should be possible and important to do much more with the liberal arts at the graduate level.

In these remarks I have, no doubt, overstated my case such as it is. I am not suggesting that a student's college education should be kept within the narrow bounds of one discipline; indeed, I would urge intensive exposure to more than one discipline. Nor am I suggesting that all work within all areas must be undertaken with intensity. I am urging that some greater emphasis be given to the possibility of earlier specialization, and that specialization itself be more broadly conceived and given greater unity within a larger discipline. I agree, of course, there are definite values to an education in common. My question is whether this idea of a community of learning cannot be further developed in the last two years of college life and also, if necessary, be somewhat modified in the earlier years to permit new unifying programs to develop. I mean to raise questions whether all the work of the first two years must be of a nonspecialized type and whether there is any necessary order from the general to the more limited as the college curriculum progresses, whether in some cases an inversion of this order might not be more profitable, and whether there is not an exciting opportunity for the development of four-year liberal arts programs developed vertically throughout the period, illuminating and including specialized studies.

I am under no illusion as to the limited importance of curricula and the greater importance of faculty and students capable of creating an intellectual community among themselves. But if any particular curriculum is not so important, the existence or the lack of existence of a viable and responsible community in

which membership signifies pressure, duties, responsibilities, and the excitement obtained from a certain
coherence seems to me to be of major significance.
One of the real glories of what is now called the
Hutchins College is that it achieved this sense of community and identification. It was inevitable, I think,
given the complexities of the modern university or
college, that this essential unity should have been
changed into something more diverse. And yet that
diversity can be reflected in a new coherence of intellectual communities with interaction and common
purpose. The university as a whole can hardly discharge its very real leadership responsibilities in the
modern world if it is not, in fact, a community of such
communities. At the very least we must make certain
that our internal structures and the organizational
beliefs of the past, which have achieved their purpose, are not hampering us from fulfilling our responsibilities.

7

The Role of a Liberal Arts College within a University

A talk given at the Liberal Arts Conference, University of Chicago
4 February 1966

In summary, the role of a liberal arts college within a university is to be a genuine part of that university, giving and responding to the other parts. Under fortunate circumstances, the college adds greatly to the university's conception of an intellectual and cultural community. The introduction of many minds into many fields of learning along a broad spectrum keeps alive questions about the accessibility, if not the unity, of knowledge. The choices made by those who are not fully committed measure the uses of scholarship, and emphasize the relationship between scholarship and practical action and the importance of contemplation and understanding. These choices encourage a reappraisal of the accustomed routine. Along the way the community has gained in interest and liveliness. The university is strengthened as an institution guiding its own growth through the persistence of questions even when the questions do not arise from the inner logic of a protected subject matter. If the college's persistence in asking "What knowledge is worth having?" creates tension or distraction—and it does—the established order on balance can nevertheless be well pleased. For the drama of the college, and a compelling drama it is, is the miraculous transformation of the bright and untutored into minds of greater power through the victory of the disciplines. But it is a victory that knows no loser, and a transformation that works its change upon the disciplines themselves.

This is an idealized account that fails to stress many of the important characteristics, problems, and paradoxes of the modern university of which the college is a part. It is difficult to describe the modern university. It is apt to be large and complicated. It is hard, in any event, to be objective about one's environment and companions. Generalized descriptions may miss the mark. The balance within one institution between undergraduate and graduate teaching, research, the carrying on of the liberal arts tradition at all levels, including the graduate and the professional, and the assumption of responsibilities and service functions may be quite different from that at another. But certain points can be made, if not for all, at least for this one.

To begin with, the range of activities is enormous. It should not be necessary to make this point about the institution which had the first self-sustaining atomic pile, which manages the Argonne National Laboratory, and which has, as an integral part of its concern, hospitals where decisions of life are made every day. The range goes from nursery schools to postdoctoral training and guidance for the professions, the development of the most intricate of laboratories, the operation of educational enterprises in Asia and Latin America, the creation of some of the most significant centers in the world for the study of non-Western cultures. There still may be some popular belief that a university is mainly an institution to which the young are sent with the hope that they will not be too visible while they are growing up.But in general the community at large knows, and perhaps knows too well, that the research and actions of the universities are often pivotal to national security, public health and order, economic and industrial development, and that the understanding of other societies which may be achieved here may determine our ability to shape a peaceful world with them.

Usefulness has invited burdens. Necessity has compelled their acceptance. We are an urban university. Because the cities, states, and federal government have not solved the problems of urban blight and urban living, the universities within the cities have become instrumentalities for redevelopment. Our campus plan becomes the means for achieving a community plan. Our conception of the university has undergone a radical change. The university is no longer an island separated from a community. There is a sense in which the community has become part of the university, imposing upon the institution the requirements that in this new relationship it avoid officiousness and the assumption of powers which it does not have, on the one hand, and on the other, that as lines of autonomy fade the institution preserve its own identity.

The range of activities and the assumption of new responsibilities impose great burdens upon the institution. Even without these burdens a university would not meet the tests imposed by a moderately responsible management expert. Most universities are not planned in the sense necessary either for a business venture or a centrally controlled eleemosynary institution. And this university is planned less than most. The management of the University of Chicago, while ultimately in the hands of the Board of Trustees, in large part resides within the faculty, organized into a federal system of ruling bodies of divisions, schools, and the college, with subruling bodies of departments, collegiate divisions, institutes, centers and committees, and an overall council. But the most important ruling body in this structure, with the greatest power and freedom, and upon whom everything else depends, is the individual professor. The gentlemen who invented the phrase "administration," or, worse still, "central administration," as applied to the University of Chicago, were either unfamiliar with the university, or possessors of a great sense of humor. Yet somehow there is sufficient coherence to marshal and still not interfere with energy and creativity. This fact is recognized by industrial firms when they praise their own laboratories as having the freedom of a university. Three factors are involved. The first is the self-selection of the faculty, whose standards and abilities derive in part from the kind of education you are receiving. The second is the impetus of the character of the institution itself, including a recognition that the system will work only with a minimum of rules and regulations. And third, through discussions more or less rational at many levels, and through ceremonies of many different kinds, the institution each day rediscovers and informally redirects its aims. This kind of self-planning, which is so important to the spirit of this institution, is not easy to achieve, but is much more compelling than may be at first recognized, and it is a priceless asset worth preserving. In these matters Chicago is aided by its comparative smallness in numbers and by its location in a living as well as a working community. In a sense there is no such thing as "after hours" at this university.

It is against this kind of background that the role

of the liberal arts college at Chicago must be examined. The college is not alone. It is a part among many. It is a most important part. It is entitled to regard itself in the same way most of the divisions and schools regard themselves, as the heart of the university. It is not in the Chicago tradition to be bashful in such matters, nor should we be. Happily our college has an appropriate sense of mission. This sets it apart from the undergraduate schools of some universities, which have lost the sense of identity and purpose once achieved by the early liberal arts colleges when they were training schools to elevate the spirits and manners of future gentlemen through the civilizing influences of the humanities, or when they were professional schools for the noble vocation of the ministry. In having a sense of mission, our college joins other portions of the university that also have an enormous sense of dedication and purpose. Our college is or should be concerned with the effects of a total educational process upon the student. This concern is shared by many of the professional schools. Of course our college is concerned with separating out the important from the trivial, and of using ideas to give meaning to facts. But this is true, or should be, through the entire university. It does not diminish the importance of the College to say that it is in good company, even though the missionary may be happiest when among the infidels.

What then gives to the college a unique role within the university? Although it also shares this function with other areas, more than any other area the college is the means for introducing the student to the university and to new subject matters. At a superficial level this means there is a time for testing and discovery to find out what the institution regards as important and to learn whether the descriptions and slogans given by the mass media to describe college life—the brilliance and maturity of the students, the indifference of the faculty, the prevalence of large lecture classes, the use of graduate students as teachers, the rules of the administration, such as "publish or perish"—are really correct. Over the country, a whole new class of professional personnel of assistant deans of students and advisers has arisen to mediate between the students and their institutions. The observations of these new professionals given in addresses at annual meetings of demi-learned societies, and apparently on any other occasion when they are allowed to speak, would confirm the worst fears that colleges are not primarily concerned with intellectual matters. The college student comes from and into a subsidized world. It is not clear to him where the subsidy begins or stops, and a subsidy presumably means that the institution has a high regard for the purpose of the subsidy. In this setting the hotel functions of the institution, the regulations of dormitory life, the location of residence halls, and the conditions of the food —always horrible—are given high priority. But these matters perhaps are really not as important as the opportunity given to the college to introduce students to the fields or structures of knowledge.

As you undoubtedly know, contrary to what is the general impression, many faculty prefer teaching undergraduates. They say that for some reason undergraduates are brighter and more intellectually responsive. I doubt whether undergraduates are brighter. Most of them become graduate students, and it is doubtful that their wit has been dulled so quickly by old age, particularly since one can see that same wit and responsiveness during the first year of a professional school. The excitement and brightness arise, I think, because of the willingness of the un-committed mind (and uncommitted is not quite the right term—unroutinized may be better) if sufficiently challenged, to test the boundaries that convention has laid down. The result can be a partnership be-tween faculty and student in which the faculty mem-ber is also challenged to try to point a path through a subject matter, or to exemplify that subject matter in the more careful view of a particular situation. This kind of movement through a discipline becomes a demonstration in intellectual honesty—a demonstra-tion that only makes its point when there is the sud-den realization that intellectual purity is not naturally within any of us. It may be, if the subject allows, that students and faculty together can explore the uncer-tain area of the application of competing general prin-ciples for purposes of practical decision—an essential kind of training for the citizen and very much in the liberal arts tradition. A college thus can become a generalizing influence within the institution, a way of communication among the disciplines, a way of restating advances of knowledge in the simplest terms, which may be the most difficult and significant terms, and a way of thinking through problem areas, with the advantage of seeing the same problem change its content and meaning as it is handled by different disciplines. I have used the term "generali-zation," but I have also been willing to link it to the handling of a very specific subject matter. I am re-minded—and, of course, it is only an analogy—of a quotation from Giacometti, commenting on the fear of many artists of painting from nature, because the painting, if realistic, would be labeled unoriginal and banal. "Actually," he said, "it's just the other way around. The closer you stick to what you *really* see the more astonishing your work will be. Reality isn't unoriginal, it's just unknown." The question, of course, is what you see, and one can see the larger in the more detailed.

I have mentioned the sense of mission that the college has. I do not believe the college can be a viable set of communities within the university without that sense of mission. The college has had an important past and a tradition of effort that has influenced undergraduate education throughout the country. There was a time when this was a monolithic program, ideally set to occur from the third year of high school through the second year of college. For various reasons, some of them accidental, this dramatic reshaping of the national pattern of the high school–college years did not occur. Instead there has been a continued upgrading of high school education. It might be possible, indeed, perhaps by lengthening the present high school programs by one year, to place the burden of the liberal arts curriculum upon them and to have the universities retreat into what would then be termed specialized or graduate programs. But this would deprive the universities of the coordinating, simplifying, and searching influence of a first-rate college program. Our college has had a brilliant past. We should build upon it. But we must recognize that in the context of the present developed structure of education, the road home is not back. We must build upon the qualities we have. This university has always been proud of its interdisciplinary character, and of its tradition of continuing and inquiring discussion that made Whitehead once describe the university as the nearest example in the modern world to ancient Athens. This was a long time ago, but we have not forgotten it. It is a tradition worth preserving. It is a tradition that the college can claim for itself. The strength of that sense of mission and tradition is exemplified by the naturalness with which this present series of discussions and seminars arose.

If the college finds its mission and its role within the univerity in this unifying and inquiring function, the college will gain the strength to fulfill this task only if the members of the faculties within the university are in fact willing to engage in undergraduate teaching in sufficient numbers. Four of the present collegiate divisions are based not only upon that organization of knowledge which has made possible the present general education courses, but on the structure beyond the departments for graduate work. The collegiate divisions thus will provide another opportunity to see whether in any meaningful way scholars in related areas find it worthwhile to develop a common or parallel treatment of subject matter. The colleges should help greatly in the development of coordinated programs at the more specialized level where these programs of necessity will go beyond departmental boundaries. For some of these tasks there is no doubt the divisional and college faculties will respond. They have already done so in great numbers. I hasten to add that I think it is a great mistake to assume that the only course worthwhile must be interdepartmental, interdisciplinary, or in some way integrating or coordinating. The fact is, however, that for many departments, courses that may meet the standards of the present general education programs can be of great help in establishing interdepartmental relationships which over time can result in much greater strength for a combined area, or which within a department can help exemplify its very principle of organization. The courses in non-Western civilization are a good example of the first; a sequence in the geophysical sciences would be an example of the latter. In my own judgment the distinction between general education courses as liberal arts courses, on the one hand, and specialized courses as nonliberal but graduate on the other, has been stultifying to the college and to the divisions. It avoids the major aspect of one basic problem of undergraduate education today, the necessity to see and develop specialized courses so that they do indeed reflect the astonishing wonders of reality within a larger intellectual setting. The failure to develop such courses ultimately will result in the failure of the general education courses as well.

The organization of the college into separate colleges under the direction and coordination of the dean and the college council will not work if these colleges do not in fact become communities with something of an existence of their own. They must become areas where communication is established between faculty and students, where ceremonies and events reaffirm the ideals of the community, and where the concern of the faculty, which is actually easily aroused, for the education of their students will give rise to those informal pressures that guide and induce faculty participation. The colleges must take hold to help develop educational and cultural programs that are outside the curriculum, and that do not take the form of

courses or any formal work, but nevertheless, or perhaps on that account, can add immeasurably to the
life of the students.

It has been one of the interesting attributes of the
university to confuse curriculum planning and structural arrangements with more basic questions dealing
with knowledge itself or with the aims of education.
Of course, the curriculum and the structural arrangements must serve the aims of education; to think of
the curriculum and the structure as ends in themselves, or somehow symbolic of the structure of
knowledge itself, has given too much rigidity to both
curriculum and structure, and has discouraged consideration and discussion of more important matters.
The need at the college level is to have the educational
mechanisms responsive to the tension between the
impossibility of knowing everything and the need to
know enough, between the demands of one field and
the importance of knowing others, between the craftsmanship of the specialist and the conversion of insights gained from the specific into the more general.
The college organization should operate to help confront the participants with these problems, encouraging new solutions, inviting new participants, and thus
in itself facilitating the process whereby both general
and specific education can become liberal.

As I understand it, this is the theory of the college
program at the University of Chicago. It is good to
know that the voices of the College are strong and
many, joining in that diversity and unity which gives
the college its special place.

8

The Seminary
and the University

Convocation address, The Jewish Theological
Seminary of America, New York
26 May 1968

This occasion suggests some reflections on the relationships—in Western culture, at least—between universities and theological schools which train for the ministry, or put differently, between the thrust or mission of organized religion and the basic principles appropriate to institutions of higher learning. One need hardly emphasize the relationships have been many and close. The transmission of culture and learning in many periods has been the particular burden and glory of the institutions of religion. This achievement has preserved cultures, fostered knowledge, and transformed the world. The flight of Rabbi Johanan ben Zakkai, at the time of the destruction of the Temple, who escaped by a ruse to the Romans and won permission to establish an academy of learning, is symbolic of the burden and the achievement. Perhaps in the tortured history of mankind this is a burden and an achievement which must be repeated many times. In our own country, many colleges and universities owe their origin to the religious impulse, to the desire to have schools to train for the ministry, to the acceptance by religious institutions of the high value of the intellectual pursuit of truth. The result, perhaps paradoxically, has been the secularization of knowledge accompanied by an enormous increase in means of communication, recording, and discovery, new levels of mass education, and what are referred to as many great institutions of higher learning separated from religious control. Perhaps this very achievement has increased the anxiety of religious orders to find a new relevance. So the setting for the relationship has changed, although perennial problems and questions remain.

The central question is the relationship between commitment and the intellectual pursuit of truth. And this, it should be said, pertains not only to the relationship between religion and theology and the universities, but within the disciplines of the university and within the religious traditions themselves. We are living in a period when in one way or another it is frequently said that "the chief function of a university should not be, as is currently assumed, the accumulation and dissemination of knowledge, but rather the encouragement of individual growth." Much is made of the propriety of irrational communication as a means of university study. An older age disparaged the collection of facts as meaningless without the support and selectivity of theory. Our time of anti-intellectualism attacks theory and knowledge itself as somehow irrelevant to social problems and individual growth. In this context there is a sympathetic confusion between the condition of what is studied and the proper intellectual tests of truth. And we are in grave danger of accepting that most malevolent of recurring dogmas: namely, that the doctrines which move men have passed the only test of truth that matters.

I do not mean to oversimplify but rather to suggest a set of common problems and by one example to illustrate their depth and complexity. There is a natural affinity between the psychological understanding of the recurring search of individuals and institutions to know or find themselves and the crisis of recognition which Martin Buber describes for the young adult. You will recall that Buber described the discovery by the young adult of the immortality of generations, "a community of blood" reaching back in time, imprinted with the sorrows and achievements of the past. And so, as he says, the Jew "will discover there still lives within him an element whose great national prototype is the struggle of the prophets against the people's straying inclinations. In our longing for a pure and unified life we hear the sound of that call which once awakened the great Essene and early Christian movements. But we also sense our fathers' fate, debasing us, in the irony of the modern Jew, an irony stemming from the fact that for centuries we did not hit back when our face was slapped. Instead, inferior in number and in strength, we turned aside, feeling tautly superior as 'intellectuals.' And this very intellectuality—out of touch with life, out of balance, inorganic, as it were—fed on the fact that for millennia we did not know a healthy, rooted life, determined by the rhythm of nature."

Now the insights in that passage are obviously many. There is reality to the collectivity which represents at the very least the traditions which shape a group. There is a rhythm—a linkage to the past. But of course Buber's essay was not just a description but a call for commitment. He was speaking of, and explicitly evoking, the forces awaiting their day. Such calls have been made at other times to different groups in circumstances not always glorious. How does one condition the call upon the mighty and often destructive forces of mankind, those mysterious and awesome movements in which hatred sometimes appears as love, coercion as a higher justice, individual guilt as lost in collective virtue or vice so characteristic of revolution? And how then does one break the rhythm through which violence and evil find imitation or justifying reaction?

Today in some areas and for special reasons the social-prophetic tradition occupies a preferred place. It is often linked not only to its positive values but to a needlessly destructive anti-intellectualism. Nevertheless, the social-prophetic tradition is in fact part of a duality—a duality of poet and scholar, commitment and reason, intuition and the logical second thought. Even in history the prophetic tradition was in some sense saved by and made possible through the opposing or complementary tradition of rabbinical scholarship and institution building. And this duality appears, as I have suggested, not only within seminaries and universities, as well as between them, but within the work of the individual scholar himself. In the same way the institutions of a civilized society, the operations, for example, of the legal system, reflect the movements for change and stability, for impulse and continuity. Institutions, like men, have grave imperfections. They are often measured by the angry because of the distance between their ideals and their practice. Yet this measure of difference, if the ideals are genuinely held, can also be the measure of their strength and value. So it is with institutions truly dedicated to learning, for here the individual mind is recognized for itself; here the works of the mind are cherished; the highest powers available to man are cultivated; here human reasoning as well as intuition finds its home. The house of learning is indeed a place for confrontation, but it is the

confrontation of minds which is called for—a confrontation in which none is vanquished, for the victory will belong to all.

My friends, I have said this much, because there
are zealots among us, as there were to prevent the
flight of Rabbi Johanan ben Zakkai, to prevent and
destroy the academies of learning. They are misguided and we should not follow them. Rather let us
seek that unity which is the unity of learning and
the unity of the human spirit.

9

The Law School
within the University

A talk given at the annual meeting of the Association
of American Law Schools, Chicago
29 December 1964

I suppose it is true that in an important sense law schools today are stronger than they ever have been. Students are becoming plentiful. A sufficient number of them are attractive, well balanced, and marketable. Three years of ordinary growth and loss of sleep will make them look the way law offices think entering law clerks should look. In some instances their geographical distribution is likely to be such as to give them good points in some employer's eyes. He likes home grown products if they are the right kind. He also likes to pull in the best from faraway places. On top of that, the lad by then may have been a law clerk to a Supreme Court justice. Many of the law students have high aptitude scores, a sufficient number to enable the quality law schools to vie with each other on their average and minimum scores in a continuous effort to convince themselves that their students are really good. The drive, imagination, and tolerance of the students are wonderful. They enable the students to relish the stimulating atmosphere of a closed society, which at times partakes of the sadistic flavor of an intellectual boot camp, and at other times is a grand theatrical performance in which every law professor is a Supreme Court Justice—U.S., that is. When the students come, they don't read or write very well. This enables law school deans to make courageous speeches on this controversial topic. It also gives the law schools something to do, for the

training which is offered is largely a training in reading and writing. Despite this training, complaints
concerning the failure of entering students to read
or write well evoke a sympathetic response from law
firms, for they know that law graduates are similarly
incapacitated. Of course, as night follows day, a certain number of law students will make the *Law Review*. From this group, future law professors will be
picked. They become full professors very fast because
they are very bright, have good aptitude scores, make
good grades, and, at the very least, were on the *Law
Review*.

I assume this partial and unbalanced description
will be taken for the loving caricature which it is intended to be. It is not easy to describe the modern
university law school—partly prep school, partly
graduate school, in part directed toward the intellectual virtues and the attributes of scholarship, and yet
in main thrust the producer of technicians for a
learned (and sometimes demi-learned) profession
containing within itself many of the same contradic-
tions and conflicts. I recall a talk, probably given for
proselytizing purposes, by a most eminent law teacher
in which he referred in a matter-of-fact way to the
"pecking order," as he described it, among the law
schools of the Ivy League. Since I was dean of one of
the greatest law schools in the world in one of the
greatest universities in the world, and that university
did not even play intercollegiate football, I was at a
momentary loss to understand what the Ivy League
business had to do with the law or law schools. I was
further puzzled because I had forgotten that his particular urban university was even in the Ivy League.
But then with the ability to reason given to me

through legal training, I realized this was the whole point. The finishing school or prep school attributes are still with us. But the result is not bad. The esprit and spirit of the modern law school are the wonder of many graduate departments and other professional schools. Indeed, recognizing the slowness with which education proceeds in the United States, we have created a liberal arts graduate program and have given to it a generalist professional thrust to justify an across-the-board attention to precision and structure within a common subject matter. We have substituted the law for the classics. We are for the most part overwhelmingly interested in teaching, which to some extent sets us apart from other graduate areas. We are giving the modern counterpart of a classical education to many who will be the leaders of our country as well as of the bar. The result is a powerful intellectual community in which a continuous dialogue is not only possible because of the sameness of subject, but is insisted upon both because of the method of instruction and the type of research which is expected and honored. The subject matter may be that of the social sciences, but we are the inheritors of the humanistic tradition. We create structures and admire them. We initiate our students into appreciation and make artists of the best of them. We write book or court opinion reviews with enthusiasm or acrid distemper which the layman misunderstands as somehow being concerned with the practical effects for good or bad of particular decisions. Poor layman. He does not understand we are artists, not social planners.

If this description has any considerable element of truth in it, I think we must agree that the modern university law school (and I realize of course that not all modern law schools are in universities) could not so well exist outside of a university environment. At the very least, the university has placed a protective cloak around the school. I think the result which has been achieved is perhaps largely unintended, or at least has not been directly faced. The motor power of course is still the thrust for the training in a profession. The bar still regards the modern law school as the successor not only in time but in spirit to the law office traineeship. The law faculties still worry most directly about the actual problems which graduates may face. The focus of law school discussions may be good, hard, tough actual problems, or problems thought to be so, no matter how far from reality they really are. But in truth this is a liberal arts education in structured reasoning. So far as subject matter is concerned, it could be cut down to two years, or, if this were really desired, it could be expanded to cover much more of the art of practice. Perhaps taking seriously the mission of the law school to train the elite citizen to participate in government within a democracy, including the governmental function of private practice, the education should—indeed must—expand to draw into itself the new knowledge of the social sciences. But change is difficult, and our skepticism, which is our stock in trade anyway, is very great. We are the victims of our own success. We have a protected oasis within the university community, and we are doing just fine. Moreover I should say at once that the law school's contribution to a university through the school's adherence to the liberal arts tradition at the graduate level—a tradition of talk and skepticism and appreciation, and the strong tradition of interest in instruction and concern for students—is very great. One can have a great university without a law school, because it has been done, but it must be much more difficult.

The modern university, mirroring many of the conditions of modern life, has changed a great deal in the last quarter-century. In the first place, it is apt to be very large not only in numbers of students and of faculty, but in the sheer number of transactions, financial or otherwise, which take place. Second, there has been an enormous change in the research environment of many universities, and to some extent what is meant by research. The large machines needed for important scientific research are expensive. A considerable portion of the budget of a university, between one-third and one-fourth in some instances, may reflect governmental support for research largely in the biological and physical sciences, and to some extent in the more behavioral aspects of the social sciences. Individual faculty become entrepreneurs for financial support and in one way or another become accountable for the time which they spend upon it. The weight of the jobs to be done and the evolving structure of the modern university encourage the pulling away of faculty groups into more or less separate entities. And this comes at a time when a whole view of the university is desperately needed. The values represented in a university are still taken for granted. Among these are the pursuit of knowledge for the purpose of understanding; the acceptance of the power of the free spirit of inquiry. But the modern condition appraises the productivity of the institution in terms of the numbers of students handled and the research which counts. This is not a conflict between the scientific and the humanistic spirit, as has been said, but a question of whether either will survive in strength the condition which has made possible the much-needed support of education and research in our day. That condition is the acceptance of the importance of education and research because of the material gains they make possible and because of their impact upon security. The inner spirit and the cultural values which provide the setting and the reason are not forgotten, but neither are they much loved for their own sake. Perhaps they never are, and yet they are all-important.

In this setting, the modern law school within a university community finds its position considerably altered. The law school as a graduate area is no longer particularly unique by virtue of its post-undergraduate status. There are many graduate areas, and graduate work is the assumed objective of a large proportion of undergraduate students. A recent study showed 26 percent of the students in some large state schools and up to 65 percent and 72 percent in other selected colleges intending to go on to do graduate or professional study. Recent studies have been interpreted also, and I don't believe them, to suggest that Ph.D. and medical students are even brighter than law students. But what this says, and we all know it, is that both some of the uniqueness of the law school by virtue of its postgraduate study and the uniqueness of the bar itself are diminishing. Lawyers after all were first important—and this was a long time ago—because they could read and write, not in the way law school deans now say they should, but barely. Now many people can read and write in the same way. Then they were unique because they were the undoubted leaders in the community. They are still among the leaders, but there are many professions which in some sense have taken over. Business itself has become a profession and is gaining strong professional and well-supported schools. The lawyer now finds himself advising clients in industry who have had more schooling than he has had and who have been back for more high-level refresher courses than are available in the law school world. Law schools are not unique either to the extent that—through their association or otherwise—they demand special recognition of their separatism, as, for example, on such an important matter as that the law library be autonomous, whatever that means. Every area of the university is apt to demand the same kind of recognition in the flurry of centrifugal forces which have overtaken the modern institution of learning. What may be unique is that the law schools have relatively less financial means to go it alone than some of the other areas. Law schools do not get large federal financial grants, and the day when law schools could operate as large tuition-receiving institutions is probably vanishing. Even the competition of the bar may not be the help to law school faculty salaries in that unique sense which may have been assumed. There is a lot of competition for physicists, mathematicians, economists, and, perhaps because of the speeches of law school deans, even English professors. I fear I am now distorting what should be the merit of the inner spirit and cultural values with somewhat crass material considerations. But if universities are to be divided up for the benefit of those areas which bring the most money or have the greatest political power, I doubt the law schools will fare very well.

These thoughts are not a newfound cloak to protect

a professor of law on leave as a central administrator. I got them, mistakenly or otherwise, as a law school dean. Indeed, I was summoned along with some of my colleagues to appear before the Legal Education Section of the American Bar Association, which has some intimate connections with your organization, to show cause, as it were, why our school should not be punished because our law library, while in fact quite separate, was part of the university system, and therefore not autonomous, and because of our recalcitrance in observing a university rule that we could not publish the separate law school faculty salary schedules. The faculty of which I was a member took the position it did because I think we realize that in the long run the strength of law schools would be greater to the extent they were part of the universities, and that separatist pressures upon universities weaken these institutions. I realize of course the public spirit and, to some extent, the provocations which have induced such separatist moves. But I suspect that at least now, or if not now, soon, the greater glory and the greater service is all the other way, and lawyers who so frequently are the guardians of the resources of our universities as well as of our law schools should be the first to recognize this.

Just as lawyers conceive of themselves as generalists and frequently are, so law professors move naturally to this same role within the university community. They come armed with a discipline and a structure of ideas covering a vast area of human knowledge and related to immediate issues of social policy. It is of course true that law, perhaps in an effort to establish itself as scientific, has often tended to make policy issues a matter of value judgments to be decided by political processes and upon which much cannot be said in any disciplined way. But the value judgments then enter into the argument anyway, even though perhaps illicitly, and the important thing is that the dialogue includes them. One might feel a little more comfortable about the role of the law schools in directing inquiry to social problems before they erupt into crises, if, for example, on such matters as reapportionment, we had been more concerned with the problem of urban and rural representation prior to the recent decisions, and were not so frequently satisfied to be only critics of the Court. Our law schools are court-tied to a considerable extent. Too much so undoubtedly. And we are talking court law when our colleagues within the university community are mistakenly grateful to us for discussing the underlying issues. They do not realize we are only talking law in a most narrow sense and of course we aren't. This suggests that somewhere within the university structure, and probably not the mission of only one school in particular, a continuing and structured dialogue ought to be fostered on important policy issues. Much of this role, indirectly sometimes and frequently directly, is performed by the law schools, and it is a magnificient and unique contribution. Law schools also have the opportunity, and sometimes they take it, to examine for law the consequences of apparent new knowledge and new techniques. One example is the research today which purports to show the overwhelming and perhaps defeating influence of early childhood environment upon later adolescence and the adult years. How should our legal institutions, fashioned for the protection of the family and also of the community, respond to these facts, if they are facts in a society which has mass delinquency and cultural deprivation? It is not I think sufficient for us to discuss only procedure and to leave the substance to some unknown other discipline to pick up. A dialogue of values—in addition to our humanistic appreciation of our artistic creations of logic—is in fact within our tradition. It is one of the things which makes us uniquely valuable to the university community.

As institutions the law schools and the universities confront each other with their own way of doing things. I suspect each could learn with profit from the other. The law schools offer an example of a community within a faculty, and including the students—a community unfortunately increasingly rare in the large amorphous university where remoteness and separatism have become the atmosphere felt by all. The university, on the other hand, increasingly backs the individual faculty member to help him go where his research runs, from one discipline to another if necessary, and without as many confining notions of what is a priori significant or achievable. The very sense of community which law schools have—and I hesitate to say this but I think it is true—has to some extent dampened the interest in new experiments and new directions by individual faculty on their own, backed up by the kind of research support which in one way or another is made available in other areas. And this indeed is strange with a subject as complicated and varied as law is, where the interdisciplinary work for one corner may be quite irrelevant in its lesson for work in another. Perhaps we should give less attention to what law schools do and give greater encouragement to law professors to do as they please. I realize, of course, this is often done, but still the results from a little bit more might be surprising.

When I was a law school dean I had to say, or so I thought, that law and law schools were of the greatest importance to the larger community and to the universities of which they are a part. Now that I am in a sense free, I find that what I said was true. I had not fully realized, however, how intertwined the roles of law school and university were, nor had I appreciated that so much of the humanistic tradition is kept alive in the professional course of liberal arts which is the law. And that is the sense of values, which while so frequently formally eschewed, helps give the law schools their distinction. It is good to hope that the values and ways of life of law schools and universities will gain from each other.

10

The Shape, Process, and Purpose of the University of Chicago

A talk given to the Class of 1971
The College of the University of Chicago
24 September 1967

There are certain characteristics which ought to distinguish a university from other institutions. There are additional characteristics which distinguish the University of Chicago. A university is old. It reflects the wisdom of man's knowledge and the error of his ways. A university is young. It reflects the excitement of discovery and understanding. A university is complex. It mirrors the search to comprehend man's nature, the social order, the very universe. A university is unified. It has a purpose. It treasures the cultural traditions of many societies so different and yet so much the same. One does not get to know a university or its work in an evening, in an orientation week, or for that matter in a lifetime. Just as a viable university must always try to know itself, so you will find your understanding of this place will grow and change, reflecting in part the change and growth which is in you. This process has already begun. It demands a mixture of zeal and patience, a mixture not easy to carry.

The University of Chicago is a university. This is reflected in the distribution of its faculty and students. Out of approximately 8,700 students, about 30 percent are in the College, 43 percent in the graduate divisions, and 27 percent in the graduate professional schools. The faculty-student ratio is about one to eight. Approximately 29 percent of the faculty of more than one thousand do some teaching in the

College. The median-size class in the College last year was between 10 and 19, which meant that many classes had more than 19 students. The graduate divisions are four: the Biological Sciences, the Humanities, the Physical Sciences, and the Social Sciences. The graduate professional schools include Business, Divinity, Education, Law, Library, and Social Service Administration. The School of Medicine is an integral part of the Division of the Biological Sciences. The university has always been careful not to spread itself thin in a myriad of vocational institutes. It sought from the start to have scholars working in the central and developing areas of knowledge. Its professional schools, all interdisciplinary in nature, have advanced the application of the intellectual arts to the problems of our society, and all of them are centers for research.

The University of Chicago began as a university, full blown, and not as a college which might later develop into a university. And because fate, greatly aided by John D. Rockefeller and William Rainey Harper, was kind, the university succeeded. It succeeded because it was an assembly of scholars unequaled in the modern world. They were confident. They were willing to try new things both in their work and in the university. Moreover, they talked to each other. The results were pioneering discoveries in the natural sciences, new comprehension of the humanities, the creation of much of the social sciences, and a flow of educational ideas which has kept the academic community on edge. This has placed an unmistakable stamp on the character of the present institution.

Certain characteristics of the present institution

are at once evident. We believe in research. Possibly the most extreme form of our faith in research was stated by Robert Hutchins when he said: "A university may be a university without doing any teaching. It cannot be one without doing any research." Mr. Hutchins was pointing to the inevitable stresses and conflicts which arise in an institution dedicated as we are to both research and teaching. If we had to choose, we would take research. Perhaps it is important to restate this faith at a time when some fear the consequences of knowledge and when others think of research as trifling fact gathering. We believe in the search to know and in its preeminence. But we have chosen—and chosen rightly I am sure —to walk the double path of teaching and research, and with emphasis on both. We welcome the conflict this imposes. We believe that research is teaching, that the new boundaries of a subject matter are among the best of ways to test old wisdom, and that good teaching is in fact discovery. We believe that the generalizing influence of teaching not only is essential to the continuation of a cultural tradition but gives new meaning and helps to position the search for knowledge. Thus, Chicago has always been proud of its College. It is a small college. It is a college which has frequently given new directions to undergraduate education. Indeed it is widely and correctly regarded as one of the three institutions which have had the greatest influence in shaping American undergraduate education. It is a college which has particularly sought to be a generalizing influence, but through the exploration of specific problems and the discussions of specific texts. It is a college which exists not only for itself but with a mission to continue to shape undergraduate education. It is a college greatly influenced by its presence within a university in which research is preeminent. Its alumni tend to continue on to professional schools or graduate work. They in turn become the leaders of professions, citizens of stature in many walks of life, the teachers of teachers. Hardly any university or college is free from their influence.

There are some interesting, even though at times painful, consequences which arise from the shape of this university. Our alumni in teaching, despite the latter-day greater affluence of the teaching profession, have less money to give us. And the costs of education at Chicago are unavoidably high. A rough approximation of the cost per student per year, without including any capital building costs at all, is $4,603. This is, of course, an average, but it understates the cost. The tuition, as you well know, is high, but happily not half that high. Recognizing the fact that income disparity among out students' families is probably greater at Chicago than at comparable institutions, Chicago returns in unendowed scholarship aid 32 percent of the tuition it receives. Special amounts for student support add greatly to this figure. Leaving out the Argonne National Laboratory, which the university operates for the U.S. Atomic Energy Commission and the Argonne Universities Association, and the Argonne Cancer Research Hospital, the budget comes to $117 million. If we leave out specially endowed funds and funds for specific purposes, the budget becomes $62 million. Omitting the hospitals and clinics, it comes to about $45 million. Looking at the regular budget in terms of the amounts which can be allocated for the College, the divisions, and the schools directly, the figure becomes approximately $30 million. The fascinating point is that to support this budget, the university must not only count on $10 million in gifts which it assumes it will receive, but an additional $4 million to come from additional gifts or out of funds functioning as endowment. We could not possibly go at this pace were it not for the gigantic drive for funds which has been mounted by the Board of Trustees.

This is the way it has been for most of the life of this university. There is a perhaps apocryphal story of Harper, who had been told not to ask John D. Rockefeller to pick up the year-end deficit any more as he had been doing for several years. Mr. Harper agreed. But when he came to see Mr. Rockefeller, Mr. Harper, since they were both religious men, suggested that they begin with a prayer. And Mr. Harper prayed mightily. In his prayer he told the Lord and Mr. Rockefeller about the financial plight of the university. He got the money. Whether true or not, there is a lot of history in that story.

The pressure of budgets has its good side. It makes us not only count our blessings but set our priorities. Our priorities are clear. We have given most emphasis to faculty salaries, scholarships, and the needs of the library. Our faculty salaries on the average are second highest in the country. I wish they could be higher. Over the last eleven years the greatest increases in the regular budget of the university have gone, with the exception of one professional school, to the College, and then to the Humanities Division. This reflects the determination of the university at a time when greatly needed scientific support has been coming in part from governmental sources, but

which in turn has been matched in considerable
amounts by university funds, not to permit a distortion of university life and goals.

Mr. Rockefeller gave more than money to the university of Chicago. He and President Harper developed the vision of a great university. Mr. Rockefeller's refusal to interfere in the operations of the
university gave the university its essential character
and freedom, in sharp contrast to many other institutions at that time. The claims of history are such
that it is well to recall President Harper's decennial
report in 1902, when he said, "I wish to add . . . that
whatever may or may not have happened in other
universities, in the University of Chicago neither the
trustees, nor the president, nor anyone in official
position has at any time called an instructor to account for any public utterances which he may have
made. Still further, in no single case has a donor to
the university called the attention of the trustees to
the teaching of any officer of the university as being
distasteful or objectionable. Still further, it is my
opinion that no donor of money to a university,
whether that donor be an individual or the state, has
any right, before God or man, to interfere with the
teaching of officers appointed to give instruction in a
university. . . . Neither an individual, nor the state,
nor the church has the right to interfere with the
search for truth, or with its promulgation when
found. . . . A donor has the privilege of ceasing to
make his gifts to an institution if, in his opinion, for
any reason the work of the institution is not satisfac-
tory; but as donor he has no right to interfere with
the administration or the instruction of the university. The trustees in an institution in which such

interference has taken place may not maintain their self-respect and remain trustees."

The work of the university is centered in the schools, the divisions, and the College. The faculties of these areas constitute ruling bodies and in general have legislative power over all matters pertaining to admission requirements, curricula, instruction, examinations, grading, and degrees. If a matter concerns more than one ruling body or substantially affects the general interest of the university, it can be acted upon by the elected faculty academic Council of the University. The academic Council in turn elects a seven-man Committee of the Council, which meets every two weeks with the president of the university. When the occasion arises, the Committee of the Council receives memorials or petitions from faculty or students on academic matters, but most of these items concern more immediately and in the first instance the ruling body of the area involved. The College has a College Council, half elected and half appointed, and its own committee which meets with the dean of the College. The dean of each area is the executive officer and the representative of his faculty. To pass from statutory language to actuality, our College in Wayne Booth* has, I believe, the best college dean in the country. Under him are the collegiate divisions, organized for the purpose of giving greater unity and direction to subject matter and to make possible further experiments to improve undergraduate education. Since you enter a collegiate division only after you have completed the first year, no master now stands between you and the dean.

I do not mean to give the impression of complete-

* Dean of the College of the University of Chicago from 1964 to 1969.

ness in this description. I have not for example mentioned the dean of students, who has important coordinating duties affecting a wide range of student
life. Last year the university academic Council recom-
mended to the president that five students be elected
and five faculty members designated to act as an advisory council to the dean of students on the wide
range of nonacademic functions performed by his
office. This recommendation was adopted by the
president. Nor do I mean to suggest that there is a
minimum of confusion in the way the university runs
itself. As a rule of thumb, one can predict that the
university with detailed rules and many procedures
will turn out to be a poor university. The spirit of a
university and the customs which reflect the care
with which faculty discharge their responsibilities
are of much greater significance. Chicago has been
fast-moving, with few rules and considerable freedom; the central purpose of the university has found
its realization in the work of the individual scholar,
in the progress of the individual student.

There is a sense in which a university has a variety
of purposes. It is an institution in the community and
shares responsibilities with other institutions. There
are a variety of housekeeping functions. If they are
performed well, they can make life more pleasant.
The university runs hospitals, legal clinics, offers
psychiatric and psychological help within the public
schools, and performs social service work. This is not
just research, but service of the highest order. The
friendship and concerns of those who live in the university community add dimensions to university
life. Nevertheless, a university over a period of time
acquires a dominant purpose and measure. This uni-

versity from its very beginning has been highly articulate and conscious of its dominant purpose and its reason for being.

The University of Chicago exists for the life of the mind. Its primary purpose is intellectual. It exists to increase the intellectual understanding and powers of mankind. The commitment is to the powers of reason. Reason is the way, the means to an end, the indispensable tool. The life of reason is a difficult life. It requires clarity, intellectual rigor, humility, and honesty. It requires commitment and considerable energy. It requires that we ask questions not only of others but of ourselves. It requires that we examine not only the beliefs of others, but those newly acquired doctrines which all are prone to believe because they are held by the group we favor, or are the cherished inspirations which come to us in the middle of the night and which we are certain cannot be wrong. One does not proceed on this path through an act of faith alone; prior innocence is no protection. Habits of thought and searching intellectual honesty must be acquired and forever renewed. The standards of excellence are demanding, and excellence is required. To comprehend our cultural traditions, to appreciate the works of the mind, to see as well as others have seen, to know and express beyond the present limits of knowledge, to preserve and open the way of reason for others—these are the goals. The path is not an easy one.

Nor is it the only path. There are many ways to the good things in life. The university is only one institution among many. We cannot be all things. We must resist the temptation to demand all pleasant things for ourselves because we would enjoy them. As the great professor Robert Redfield said some years ago: "A university that represents itself as just like other agreeable places to spend time either is no university or is deceitful. A true university cannot reflect the total society in its tastes and interests. It has made a somewhat different emphasis in choosing among the many goods open to man." We must resist also the well-intentioned demands which are made upon us which would make us just another social or governmental agency. We must acknowledge that there are doubters—possibly some among you—and all of us at times are afflicted with these same doubts, concerning the life of reason and the life of action in these troubled times. Universities have often existed in troubled times, and often, including in this half century, when faith in reason has been lost. But the faith of a university and its inner integrity are never more important than in such periods of doubt.

I join with others in welcoming you to what we trust will be an exciting period of discovery and to that growth which will win for you the highest powers of man.

11

Unrest
and the Universities

A talk given at a meeting of the Life Insurance
Association of America, New York
11 December 1968

Some aspects of university life are now high on the list for popular discussion. The described conduct appears to ask what kind of people we are or are becoming, what kind of society we have and what is to become of it? Unrest in the universities is trivialized if it is not seen in a larger and contemporary context.

Of course, there is another dimension. If unrest is taken as a euphemism for what is regarded at the time as misconduct, there has been plenty of it in universities from the beginning. The uproarious conduct of faculty and students, and town and gown disputes, closed medieval and renaissance universities and sometimes created new ones. In our own country Thomas Jefferson in 1823, thinking about his newly founded University of Virginia, said the rock he most dreaded was the discipline of the institution. "The insubordination of our youth," he wrote, "is now the greatest obstacle to their education." He sought the advice of Professor Ticknor of Harvard on the handling of dissatisfaction, disobedience, and revolt. Ticknor publicly had one bit of advice among others: "The longest vacation should happen in the hot season, when insubordination and misconduct are now most frequent." Fifty years later a prominent American professor of English, comparing German and American universities, thought it relevant to point out that the German professor's "temper is not ruffled by the freaks or downright insults of mutinous youth."

When unrest centers around political issues of the society, we may console ourselves by remembering one tradition of thought which held it simply impossible to educate young people in such matters. "A young man," wrote Aristotle, "is not a proper hearer of lectures on political science, for he is inexperienced in the actions that occur in life. . . . Further, since he tends to follow his passions, his study will be in vain and unprofitable because the end aimed at is not knowledge but action." Aristotle made it plain he was talking not only about the young in years but also about the "youthful in character." In his old age Plato had a number of solutions for the political propensities of the young. "Assuming you have reasonably good laws," he said, "one of the best of them will be the law forbidding any young man to inquire which of them are right or wrong; but with one mouth and one voice they must all agree the laws are all good." He thought an old man might criticize the laws, but only "when no young man is present."

But the consolation of history does not work. All crises of unrest speak to their own time. Ours speaks to us. It is a warning of failures, although perhaps not always the specific failures the dissidents have in mind. To say the manifestations of unrest have the significance of warnings, and thus have meaning, is not to characterize them, in one of the current platitudes, as simply another form of communication. That suggests that the means chosen for the message are not as important as the reasons for dissatisfaction. But this is not necessarily true. We have to find out what is significant and important in both the means used and in the fact of dissatisfaction. This is not the same as looking for the causes or reasons for unrest. The human condition and aspirations being what they are, dissatisfaction is to be expected and nurtured. It is the particular form and manifestation which become important, as well as the failure of institutions of society to guide, respond to, or relate effectively to the force of discontent.

While I accept the significance of university discontent as a way of looking at problems of the society at large, this way of looking has its own distortion. The university has its closest relationship with a particular segment of the community, not only in part a population of the young, but also one which is more concerned with words and symbols. Universities are often regarded as mirrors for the larger society. Philosophers of social reconstruction frequently deny the power of their own thought to change the image, perhaps as a way of asserting the validity of their perception. So John Dewey, urging the social reconstruction of the nation in 1929, wrote, "Literary persons and academic thinkers are now, more than ever, effects, not causes." But the interrelationship between the world of ideas and the facts of life is intricate. The university is or should be the home of ideas. Ideas are properly subversive, frequently wrong. They give power to see correctly and also, of course, to see incorrectly. On the level of ideas there is both a special responsiveness within the university community and also a stubborn selectivity. For related reasons there is vulnerability on the part of the university to certain forms of discontent. But these distortions help to magnify and thus to identify some of the problems of the society at large. They may help to identify our failures.

Our most pressing failure relates to our attitude toward the legal system. Civil disobedience and indifference to law have become sufficiently widespread to reflect and raise essentially naïve questions as to the function of law in a modern society. It is paradoxical that the civil rights movement, which in the almost immediate past built upon the force of law and depended so much on the morality of acquiescence, should now, to some extent, be the vehicle for the destruction of this acquiescence. The undeclared Viet Nam war has further emphasized the morality of illegal acts. It is, indeed, difficult to speak of the protest movements without appearing either to augment an alarmist view or to minimize or deny their cause. The fact is, they have occurred, and there are continuing consequences for the legal system. For some, these events have endorsed illegal protest as a way of life. Justification is felt or found in the sense of injustice, in history, and in doctrine. So there is recollection of the illicit in the obdurate conflicts of the labor movement, or the compulsion of law is equated with colonialism. And there is excitement, the sense or fact of accomplishment, which stands as a criticism of the lack of public goals within the life of conformity. One is reminded of the description of Britain at the time of the Suez crisis. "There was . . . a current wave of nostalgia for the last war, a sense of the boredom and fatuousness of contemporary Britain: it was the year of *Look Back in Anger*. . . . Nearly everyone seemed touchy, and when the Canal was seized there was an instinctive feeling that something must be done. There was a mood of almost tribal recidivism, like the moods that sweep through a school, which was not easy to resist."

But it is ancient wisdom that at some point violations of individual laws can greatly impair the shield necessary for the future welfare of the community. The burden upon the legal system has been substantial.

Our legal system would have been in difficulty without this added burden. The increasing size of our communities is but one factor in making intolerable certain abuses or inadequacies which long ago should have been corrected. Consider a legal system which insists protest will be protected and need not cross the line of illegality, and yet compels the violation of law, with all the risks for the individual and the community which must accompany this, as the only road for testing the constitutionality of many statutes. Or a legal system which operates with a schedule of fines imposed without regard to the ability of the defendant to pay. Or a system which perpetually proclaims that justice delayed is justice denied, but accepts unconscionable delays, with the personal hardships this causes, as a necessary fact of life. Or a system which only in the last few years has moved to correct the vice of using poverty as a screen against the effective raising of defenses in criminal cases. These examples are perhaps not as important in themselves as they are tests of the sensitivity of the system to the kind of lesson it teaches. Viewing the legal system in its larger dimension, as one must, one finds lessons also taught by inadequate or abusive policing in urban areas, the misconduct of legislative committees, the passing of vindictive or unconstitutional laws, or the strange, sometimes called "political," conduct of prosecuting attorneys.

It is inadequate to respond to this picture by saying that it describes life in the United States, which is, after all, pretty good. The description is of official action of the instruments of law. The operation of the legal system—for good or bad the greatest educational force in our society—inevitably creates a picture of the kind of community we would like to have. In this sense it either represents and speaks to our better selves or it carries a message of indifferent power or worse. The current unrest questions the persuasiveness of this system. Part of our difficulty perhaps arises as a concomitant of excessive reliance on judicial interpretation of the constitution. This may have weakened, as some have said it would, the thrust for legislative improvement of the system as a whole. Excessive reliance on changing constitutional doctrine creates other difficulties, increasing the sense of injustice by expectations which are then unfulfilled. The extension of constitutional doctrine sometimes carries a technical message where proper conduct and fairness should have been consciously resolved outside the courts as an issue of policy. But it is plainly wrong to blame the courts for what is chiefly the weakness of legislative and executive action. The problems of policy go beyond the structures we now have. We have to take account of the complexity of our cities, and to provide the forums, both judicial and legislative, perhaps places also for citizens' debate, which can win a personal response— a response upon which the magic of the legal system depends. In our own thinking we have to put civil rights and property rights together again. We need, in short, the organizing view of a jurisprudence.

This jurisprudence will have to speak to the current popular view of power and coercion. This is an extraordinary transformation of what was once accepted as the powers and responsibilities of citizens and officials in the American tradition. The transformation not only assumes what some of us surely regard as quite false, that a necessary and desirable aim in life is power over others, but it sees coercion in all relationships, including the coercion of benefits. It then equates power with violence, assuming that violence within an established system is simply not separately recognized. What the conception does, in a fairly standard way, is to deny the legitimacy of governmental authority, or governmentally derived authority. It may or may not substitute some special human quality or condition as an alternative to that authority, and it may or may not impose some other restriction on violence. I mention this because this view, although perhaps not with all its implications, is furthered by a number of factors: the widespread use of the idea of the power structure itself; the undoubted influence of the manifestation of violence in international life coupled with the characterization of the United States as the primary power; the picture of government officials finding their fullest satisfaction in the manipulation of power; and the belief that in an affluent society choices are not severely limited by necessity. The view is also furthered by the assumption there are safeguards in the intention, motives, or depth of feeling with which power is exercised. As I write these words, I am haunted by an illustration used by Paul Tillich to describe the union of love and power. "We read that in the Middle Ages, during the trial and execution of a mass murderer," Tillich wrote, "the relatives of the murdered fell on their knees and prayed for his soul. The destruction of his bodily existence was not felt as a negation, but as an affirmation of love. It made the reunion of the radically separated soul of the criminal with himself and with the souls of his natural enemies possible." There is relatively little comfort in this dreadful tale.

The preoccupation with power and coercion undoubtedly reflects, as I have suggested, justified criticism of what appears to many as the central position given to power in our national vision. A society requires a vision of its better self. The legal system and other institutions serve to create it. One wonders what ours now is. We have not adjusted to the impact of new forms of communication or the intensity and immediacy with which all forms of communication can now operate. Our infirmities are there enlarged; our difficulties are endlessly, and frequently erroneously, explained. Yet what is portrayed, and even the arguments made, are not really strange to American history. Violence, the tension among groups, the domination by machines—these are themes ancient as our history runs. But something has happened to our understanding. It is, indeed, surprising that a society as much concerned with the crisis of identity of groups and of individuals should have failed to be more successfully introspective with regard to itself. It is this apparent lack of coming to terms with what we are which becomes the stated justification for confrontation. Yet we do recognize our current difficulties. What we fail to acknowledge or articulate is the imperfections and limitations in man himself—all men, young and old—imperfections which give rise to the necessity of living together in certain ways and under certain understandings. We have lost coherence and eloquence about our common condition, what is good that is here and what we wish to become. It is not at all true that the way things are stated makes no difference. We have relied on forms of speech and perhaps of thought which are essentially degrading. Thus, one does not ask those who riot to cease doing so because they are chiefly hurting themselves and not others, or ask the community to do what it ought to do because if it does not there will be more riots and more destruction. This is not to assume that eloquence will carry its own implementation. But in fact it will help greatly. We have all been warned of the frustrations of promises, the awkward thud created by the dropping of goals stated in presidential task forces, the hollow ring of the promises of legislation. There is very little in these to win the commitment of a citizenry or to unify a society. The problem of the cities, of course, will remain. But one can evoke a difference—an approach more effective, more embracing. There is nothing which decrees that areas which need the most must be given the least. We are an idealistic people, and it is quite likely there will be a response. In any event, we were told a long time ago that the penalty for no vision is severe.

Disruption in the universities now reflects a weakening in the persuasive power of law. It reflects also an erosion of the discipline of the protest movements. The civil rights movement, when it created the climate of protest, for the most part made its case upon the lawfulness of its conduct. It was a step beyond, when conduct with no serious claim to legality was chosen

to force confrontation. Yet even here civil disobedience required a special acquiescence in the idea of law.
Civil disobedience, in terms of its own structure of
justification, is a form of witnessing, an appeal to
higher values; and it has required, as a confirmation
of the nature of the act, that there be a willingness,
indeed a desire, to accept the penalty for its violation
of law. But this tradition has become ineffective as
disruption itself becomes a primary aim and goal. This
general or eclectic disruption is, apparently, to be
taken as an attack upon society itself; a criticism
through a kind of caricature of what is viewed as society's preoccupation with power and its manipulation; an imitation and adoption of the aggression
which is protested. The references to particularly
aggressive political figures of a past generation are
frequent.

The universities are viewed as a part of the political society. They are regarded as an arm of the state
because their work is important or necessary to the
state's welfare. Moreover, the universities are thought
to be used by the state to achieve the technological
advances necessary for all kinds of power, including
military; to feed the economy with trained persons,
and also for the purpose of keeping young people out
of the labor market. Whether the university is public
or private—the argument goes on—it receives money
from the federal government and, like everything else
in our society, is affected with a public interest. Its
claim to freedom is then regarded as an unfounded
assertion of special privilege. Like all institutions and
persons it is subject to coercion, and uses power—it
is said. Thus, the view is that it has coerced its students by attracting them with the benefit of essential

training, and by being part of a society in which the
selective service system puts pressure upon students
to stay in school. It is, indeed, a community in which
the student expects to spend many years. If he leaves,
he will go to another one, said to be just like it, for,
generally speaking—the rhetoric claims—the communities are interchangeable. Any argument that
there are different kinds of institutions, and that the
student voluntarily chose this one, is thought to forget the coercion he is said to be under, and, in any
event, is like telling a citizen of a country he can go to
some other place. The institution's denial of certain
kinds of power is then regarded as either hypocritical
or an impossible attempt to abdicate responsibility,
like the unconcerned citizen.

The central charge is that the institution is part of
the political order and a proper target for politicizing.
This view is furthered by politicians or statesmen
who may not only view the universities much as the
students do, but who also see the protesting as a kind
of reflection—or at least so they hope—of their own
interest. So the protests within educational institutions in Great Britain are translated by a member of
the House of Commons into his own terms. He writes:
"Not all students I hope are content simply with a
choice between Mr. Wilson and Mr. Heath every
five years. Not all students, as they contemplate an
actual fall in the standard of living in this country
and the appalling situation through famine in India
or through war in Nigeria (where socialist-capitalism
is improving the balance of payments by selling
arms), accept that British bureaucracy is the answer
to the world's trouble. They believe they could do
better." The revolt, then, can express a variety of dis-

satisfactions, avoiding the failure—and this is the illustration so frequently used—of the German professors to protest the rise of Hitler. As to this, Professor Dawson of Harvard has written: "Some memories are short. German universities in 1933 were occupied by storm troops, wearing brown shirts, not blue jeans. The German universities became instruments of political and social action and served their masters well." The Dawson argument would not be regarded as particularly cogent. It would be said that almost anyone should be able to distinguish good political ends from bad ones.

All this may well lead to the conclusion that it is good that disruption and unrest have found their way to colleges and universities because, after all, it is a problem for education. And yet for this very reason it is a peculiarly difficult problem for education to deal with. The movements tend to reject reason, which is the way of education. They buttress this rejection by replacing reason with personal qualities thought to be more than adequate substitutes. As always, the corruptions of thought come home to roost. Moreover, coercion and disruption are, in fact, offensive to the very idea of a university. For this reason a university is most vulnerable to them. Over a long period of time it cannot live with them, and to the extent that they are present, they diminish and deteriorate the quality of the institution. And this comes at a time when the quality of intellectual life in our institutions is under attack in any event.

It is not certain there is an answer. But obviously the attempt has to be made. One would hope it can be most appropriately made through a patient reassertion of the universities' own conception of themselves as places for disciplined thought, as academies of the mind, as custodians of our culture, the restorers of eloquence, and the centers of that intellectual concern and unrest which can change the world.

12

Values in Society: Universities and the Law

A talk given to the American Law Institute, Washington, D.C.
23 May 1969

As with all crises, the turbulence in our universities tells us about ourselves. It reveals the odd position which universities occupy. It portrays something of how law is regarded and reflects what law has been doing. It underscores traits, beliefs, and conditions of our society. In this conflict the universities are attacked not only because they are available and easy targets, but in part because they are regarded as among the controllers of values. They are viewed as instruments of power in the service of the social order —involved in the disbursement of public funds, the exercise of the royal privilege of defining the public good, the control over the lives of the young by shaping their minds and channeling careers. A chief tactic against them has been an aberrant form of civil disobedience which feels less need to confirm its witness to an injustice by welcoming or accepting punishment. Perhaps this is because the tactic finds its greater meaning in a generalized protest against society and the coercion of its laws. Some people find comfort in this because they regard acts of aggression against institutions of learning as particularly offensive. They would prefer an explanation which shows the real target elsewhere.

Universities are not the major controllers of value in our society. Law, itself, for better or worse, and including the public's view of its operations, is perhaps the chief educational force. An older civilization recognized this primary purpose and power. "Legislators make the citizens good by forming habits in them," Aristotle wrote, "this is the wish of every legislator, and those who do not effect it miss the mark, and it is in this that a good constitution differs from a bad one; the things that tend to produce virtue taken as a whole are those of the acts prescribed by the law . . . with a view to education for the common good." The compulsion of the law was important, "for most people obey necessity rather than argument and punishments rather than the sense of what is noble."

Admittedly this is a broad view of the law which also emphasizes its administration. Both the broad view and law in its specific application seem particularly relevant when issues of policy concerning civil disorder or civil disobedience are determined. It is particularly distressing, therefore, to find that the commissioner of education and the attorney general publicly differ in their view of campus disorders—the commissioner stressing his concern for underlying causes and linking his praise for the younger generation with a forecast of "growing unrest on the campus" for some time to come; the attorney general strongly condemning some of the participants and their disruptive behavior. The commissioner explains that this difference is not important because the attorney general is only looking at the matter from the point of view of enforcing the law. This split approach —if that is what it is—is not helpful to the thoughtful and effective administration of justice or to the understanding of campus disruptions, which probably have their greatest significance because they result from and help to create an attitude toward the legal system, and which, if they are not understood in this way, can have widespread effects upon that system and throughout our society.

The protests do mirror various aspects of the larger society. They reflect historic tendencies in American culture. They imitate, in their own way, recent events —sometimes literary events—which have made an impact. The protests have now gone on long enough so they have developed something of a culture and style of their own. It should be possible, despite the ambivalence which many share, to describe in a sketchy way what the prototype looks like.

The protests, as befits the inheritors of the American way, are frequently conducted with great technical skill and energy, building upon what appears initially to be very little support, and yet finally achieving a large event. Committees are formed. Issues are found and tried out. Symbolic action, frequently involving some kind of confrontation and perhaps a certain vituperation, is used to build support. It is a time of testing. Doctrines and slogans have already been accepted. They gain strength by being linked to national or international issues where there is injustice or frustration, or to something which happened at some other university. The institution is viewed as an imperialist power. There is close cooperation with the public communications media. The pace quickens. The oratory sometimes has a resemblance to speaking in tongues. It is a kind of canting. Picketing or similar events are arranged to keep things moving. If the issues seem right, nonnegotiable demands are presented. If possible, a building is seized. It is viewed as liberated. Endless meetings and activities are now held in it.

The entire event is seen as enormously important, and there is much excitement. Within the building there may be a feeling of unity and new comradeship. There is some fear the police may be called, and perhaps a few of the participants desire they should be. A negotiating committee has been appointed. The issues now begin to change somewhat. The list grows longer. Items on the list disappear, or it is said they are no longer to be taken seriously. The point is made that there may be a reasonable argument for some of the items. The institution is told it ought to be listening and at the same time be sufficiently understanding not to take what is said literally. Distinctions are now made as to appropriate and more inappropriate conduct. The seizure is described as peaceful and nonviolent. Amnesty has been demanded. The labor union negotiation analogy is pushed. Mediation is suggested. There may be some kind of escalation of conduct later regarded as particularly unfortunate. Most such protests come to an end in one way or another. The building is returned. Sometimes a special effort is made to clean it up. The variations in the prototype are enormous. The police may have been called. Injunctions may have been obtained. There may be court cases. There may be discipline within the institution. There may be a combination of all three and added possibilities. There may be nothing but utter confusion. It is probable that there is a demand the university be restructured. The scars are much deeper than one might imagine. And, of course, there are other consequences. Meanwhile, there are many expressions of gloom or comfort to the effect that with the problems of the world the way they are, this kind of activity must be expected to recur.

I have purposely understated the dangers, the harm, the immediate traumatic and the long-term searing effects. There is no single rule for the best handling of these events. But I think this much can be said. Particularly because these festivals are built upon a conception of the world ruled by coercion and corruption, the university's response must exemplify the principles which are important to it. The university must stand for reason and for persuasion by reasoning. Reasoning of this kind requires a most difficult honesty—an intellectual discipline which is self-critical. It is most unfortunate and in the long run disastrous for a university to exemplify expediency which avoids or solves conflicts by the acceptance of ideas imposed by force. So the university must show that it values and respects the individual mind, that discussions can always proceed, but that a threat to the disciplined freedom of the university is a threat to its very existence and purpose. This approach requires candor, consistency, and openness, but also effective discipline. The discipline will be difficult. But the university owes this much to itself, and it also owes this much to the larger society.

The disruptions must be seen against the background of not only what has happened in our colleges and universities, but also in the larger society. There are more young people. More of them are going to college. More of them intend to go to graduate and professional school. There is a long road of what appears to many of them as confinement in education ahead of them if they are not drafted. They

view themselves as quite a separate generation—
quite different from the days of World War II when
Churchill could speak of the same generation being
involved in two world wars; a generation now has a
span of four or five years. They have been told and
they believe they are members of a most affluent
society—a society which has failed to do its duty in
the correction of social evils. There is a special reason why two failures seem very close to them. The
undeclared Viet Nam war is seen not only as a catastrophe of foreign policy, but also as a peculiarly
generational war—their generation—because so
much of our society is not involved in it at all. There
is no passion of shared sacrifice within the larger
community. Many of the colleges and universities
are in cities. The urban crisis is a reminder of racial
inequality. Steps to correct this have increased the
awareness of injustice. They are reminded of past
unlawful conduct under the cover of the legitimacy
of law. Both the Viet Nam war and the continuing
inequalities appear to them as examples of power and
coercion where civil disobedience, if one feels sin-
cerely, can be justified.

They have been brought up under the barrage of
new forms of communication which have surrounded
them with images which replace, block out, and substitute for experience. They believe a great deal of
what they have been repeatedly told. They think the
generation of their parents was only interested in
material matters. They believe their own awareness
is a first step to the solution of problems, although in
the strange rhythm of history many of the means
which they are willing to employ were used in a prior
time by people and in movements they would find

most hateful. One hopes that Burke's comment in his essay on the French Revolution will not be applicable: that those who think they are waging war with intolerance, pride, and cruelty . . . are authorizing and feeding the same odious vices. They have been told, as the commissioner of education stated, "This is the finest young generation we've ever had. . . . The young people are capable, they're bright, they're knowledgeable, they know more than any generation." But in a protective society where they see only errors and not the reality of choice, their experience in doing has been long delayed. The colleges have found it difficult to build upon common experiences; they have not given these students, by and large, a training in the liberal arts. Students often have not yet developed the intellectual skills to solve the problems which concern them. Many of them are possessed by a sense of collective guilt. They are not living up to their own standards, which are high, and they have been denied—again one wonders at this rhythm of history—the terrible but complete experiences of depressions and wars in which one had to prove oneself. For many the disruptive experience is symbolic of what is sought.

In a real sense, a catastrophe or an overwhelming collective and personal experience is sought. Many of these sentiments are shared with or encouraged in them by the various ministers of the churches and synagogues which surround the universities. Love is opposed to power and reason. The natural sciences do not offer "means of understanding what are essentially human problems"—do not show the causes of what went wrong—so that mankind is burdened with an "evil past legacy"; but the humanities and

the social sciences also do not give to us a "ruth-
lessly honest analysis of existing social evils, but a
framework in which problems are defined in terms
of the existing culture." This is what many read and
this is what many feel. In another day religious
orders might have provided an avenue for service.
Despite the Peace Corps, Vista, and the interest of
the churches, insufficient avenues of this kind have
been created.

The struggle, then, is over the nature of the university. I have mentioned the odd position which
universities now occupy. The position is a precarious
one. The normal complaints about the academic performance of universities, the preoccupation with research, the neglect of teaching, the large classes—
these usually are not that important, at least for
many places where the protests have arisen. There is
no doubt that education should be greatly improved.
The required years of study ought to be shortened.
They can be. We should reduce the number of years
made standard for higher education—years which
are stultifying and delaying for so many—and we
should do this in part in recognition that education
is a continuing process which should be renewed
in various ways throughout the adult years, and also
because it is sinful to waste educational resources
when they are so badly needed at the preschool, primary, and secondary school levels. There is no reason
why entrance to law school, for example, should be
postponed until after graduation from college. The
three years required for law school, as an optional
matter, could be reduced to two. We could take
much more drastic steps than that with benefit to
all. We should search for more points of entrance

and exit with honor from the system so that we would not be removing from society for so long a sustained period a substantial segment of the population. A great deal of graduate work should be curtailed by making a doctor's degree less necessary for teaching.

The struggle, I think, will not be so much over these matters, but over the basic freedom of these institutions to pursue their work as they determine it, and as teaching institutions to give training to students in the disciplines of thought, the appreciation of cultures, the criticism of reason. Whatever their origin, whatever their peripheral activities, whatever the reason for giving support to them may have been, it is these qualities and this freedom, sometimes—usually—hard won, which have given to our universities their basic quality and their true value. But now the universities find themselves urged, almost compelled, to engage in increasing service activities—to act as agencies for the restoration of cities, to give one example. The euphoria is catching. The possible appropriateness of a subject for research, its importance for discussion, is confused not only with the actual accomplishment of significant research, which does not happen so often, but also with superior ability and the institutional power to solve and manage social problems and to determine national policies. And so the protesters say, "Why not act for us to compel the adoption of a different foreign policy?" The universities see themselves viewed as necessities, if not for the education of all youth, then at least as channels and screens through which all must pass. They hear themselves described as "the central institution of the next hundred years" because of their role "as the source of innovation and knowledge." It is doubtful if institutions so regarded will be able to retain their freedom. The current controversy over the governance of universities is probably only a pale image, if not already the doorway, for what is likely to come. If the universities are to become a kind of mirror image of the political order, then we will have to develop new institutions weak enough to be free, but in which ideas can be developed which are strong enough to change the world.

But law, as I have suggested, is the greatest educational force. It teaches through its administration of justice. It teaches—for better or worse—through the police, through the conditions of the cities, of the public schools, and of the courts themselves. It teaches through its sometime neglect of civility and its occasional endorsement of apparent cruelty. It teaches through example, compulsion, and the effective concern to create institutions, to perfect measures, to get jobs done—which is the organizing special noble responsibility of the bar. Today, more than in any recent time, there is great importance that these jobs be done. The trust in the fabric of law needs to be restored. The message of a jurisprudence that works needs to be conveyed. Whatever the meaning of these disruptions, here is the answer which will make the most difference.

13

The Purposes of a University

Convocation address, University of Rochester
7 June 1969

In these days of anguish, this occasion presses the university to judge itself. Education, when it is at its best, is both a disruptive and a fulfilling process. The question-asking is never ended. We pretend, at least, to welcome these questions. We must do so now.

Perhaps this is a transition time in our history—one of those rare moments, which in a more subdued form come to every generation, when there is a jolting recognition of dissatisfaction with the way things are. It is as though we had returned from some deep sleep to a society we know is our own, but is different from what we expect, with directions we do not understand, with problems we think should have been solved. At such a time we are fearful of the history which might explain if not justify. We separate ourselves from the debates, the strategies of another era. We find delays intolerable. We are caught by the persistence of war in Viet Nam, by the long-term effects of racial discrimination at home. This pretended separation from the past does not protect us from a feeling of collective guilt—the invention "of a sort of pedigree of crimes"; indeed, it renders us more defenseless. So positioned, we look at society filled with luxuries for some, including most particularly ourselves. We recite a commonplace of evils—each the object of reform, properly documented by a White House task force or legislative committee, endlessly reported by the communications media which rule our lives. In this way, serious problems requiring choice, effort, and sacrifice are made banal. Impatience as well as repetition is easy to come by. Our generations are not the first to cry the world is too much with us, nor are we the first to hear violence justified. There is a rhythm of history in these matters. But this is the time of our awareness.

We regard education with ambivalence. Education is identified with an institution or with a system. Institutions and systems are defined as unresponsive to the wishes of the individual. They are bureaucratic and impersonal. Our education has told us so. Along with the cult of the personal—the lecturer does not know my name—our society is witnessing a wave of anti-intellectualism. The educational system is scorned not only for mere fact gathering or stuffing, which is a traditional complaint, or for being part of the knowledge industry, which is our own invention, but for an overemphasis on reason with its false objectivity and its arrogant claims to understanding the human condition. As in somewhat similar periods in other countries, the educational system is accused of neglecting personal values, failing to speak to the needs of the individual and of the society. One is reminded of the platform of that most infamous of all political parties in Germany demanding that the curriculum of all educational establishments be brought into line with the requirements of practical life. Yet withal, there probably has never been a time when education on a mass scale was more highly valued. It is assumed that education can do almost anything if properly controlled.

In this setting, colleges and universities are a special case. They have been hard pressed. The significance of the view that colleges and universities have limited functions—there are many other kinds of social and public agencies—is no longer accepted. Higher education is said to be a necessity, a gateway to industry and to a career. The institutions are regarded as screening devices, sorting people out according to their abilities or credentials, creating certified status. More young people than ever before go to these institutions. The whole educational system has grown longer in time, larger in size. The size of the institution is confused with strength. The undergraduate college has become a common inn, taking the place in the last stages of education once occupied by the high school. The college, itself, is regarded as preparatory to the expected graduate or professional programs. Along with these changes, and because public funds have come to students, faculty, and institutions, the distinction between public and private education is blurred. Some would say it has disappeared.

Colleges and universities suffer from their pretense to excellence, universal ability, and power. They jump from the fact that a relatively few scholars over long periods of time have had ideas which have changed the world, to the notion that the institutions themselves are the important engines of social change, capable not only of having and understanding ideas, but of carrying them out in the practical order. Since social change, in fact, occurs, of course innumerable institutions, professions, and groups in our society play a role in that change and are touched by it. But there is an enormous and erroneous temptation to jump from the spectaculars of the applied group work of science to the assumption that this kind of strength is the normal and proper attribute of the teaching research institution which is a university. With some exceptions, most training in the applied fields is better off outside the universities, and most of the applied work of science is better conducted outside the universities.

The assumed importance of universities for a particular kind of national strength is disconcerting. One must be concerned with the implications of the possibly playful remark of an eminent university scientist. He said: "The government can't afford not to support us. Would a man commit suicide in that way, by cutting himself off from the information he needs?" This statement might sound reassuring. It is quite the opposite. One wonders whether the universities, in fact or in fancy, have become so useful, so important, so necessary that they have lost themselves.

It should not be asserted there is one prototype for the perfect university. Over time, universities have taken many forms and fulfilled many purposes. There is, and there should be, considerable diversity among them. The judgment of the basic contribution and impact of these institutions as a whole upon our life and culture is not easy to make. It will evoke much disagreement. For a good deal of their history in this country many colleges have been highly regarded because they gave a kind of custodial care, helped young people to learn to adapt, provided entertainment and some exercise in the world of sports. But in fact, even these institutions usually had more important virtues. Today the conception of a university is baffling in its complexity and lack of central

purpose. We must try to regain an understanding
of what that central purpose is.

Universities and colleges have kept alive the tradition of the life of the mind. They have continued
the traditions of culture and rediscovered cultures
which had died. They have inculcated an appreciation for the works of the mind, developed the skills
of the intellect, emphasized the continuing need for
free inquiry and discussion, the importance of scientific discovery, the need to understand the nonrational. Thus they have stood for the concept of the
wholeness of knowledge, for the morality of that intellectual criticism which is so difficult because it is
self-criticism, requiring the admission of error. They
have helped to create a thoughtfulness about values.
They have held to the conception that these skills,
this appreciation, this examination of values, this
way of inquiry are the possession of the free man to
be acquired through education. This is what a liberal
education is about, and its illumination is essential
if graduate and professional work are to participate
in the intellectual tradition.

It is true this is an idealized picture if applied to
any single institution, and somewhat absurd if applied to many. But it describes a central thrust carried forward at particular times by enough scholars
and enough institutions to have had a pervasive influence. It is an approach to education which emphasizes the magic of a disciplined process, self-
generating, self-directing, and free from external
constraints. An approach which requires an inde-
pendence of spirit, a voluntary commitment. It forces
the asking of questions. It is not content with closed
systems. It is not committed to the point of view of

any society. It does not conform to the ancient and now modern notion that education is here to carry out the ideas and wishes of the state, the establishment, or the community. Thus, it is opposed to the view that education is good if properly controlled. Again, for a variety of reasons, the ideal is beyond reach. The attempt is important and makes the difference. It is sometimes said that society will achieve the kind of education it deserves. Heaven help us if this is so. This approach seeks to do better.

This view of the central purpose of higher education is probably a minority position. Everyone thinks he knows that what goes on in educational institutions is frequently far different: the undergraduate's losing battle against prerequisites and sliced-up courses; the graduate and professional training programs which have little to do with discovery or understanding; a hierarchy of values largely unexamined; research which has become a service function. Thus the university is criticized not because it engages in activities which have little to do with the life of the mind—this is accepted as appropriate—but because it has chosen to serve the wrong masters and has not harnessed its powers to do good. And universities are graded on prestige factors—the number of books in the library, the number of graduate degrees conferred, the proliferation of research projects—which at least would be seen in a new light if the university's central purposes were taken as an organizing principle. But the reason for emphasizing the intellectual tradition of the life of the mind is not because that is what most frequently goes on in universities. Rather it is because the life of the mind in the university makes the most difference.

Other institutions can do many other important things just as well or even better. They should be encouraged to do so.

In this time of awareness, universities must examine what has happened to them—what their relationship should be to changed conditions. We have developed the longest system of higher education the world has ever known. More students expect to go to graduate and professional schools than ever before. Among the professions there has been a race to see which could require the longest amount of training. We have taken subject matter which was once handled in a challenging way at the undergraduate level and moved it to the later graduate and professional years. Much graduate education has little or no relationship to the purposes which it is supposed to serve. A great deal of it is gone into solely because a doctor's degree has been made a requirement for teaching—an objective for which much doctoral training has an almost disqualifying relationship. We have made a fetish about the quantity of research. Although it may be a kind of treason to say it, not all that much research is all that important. In lengthening the process and postponing so much of the training to the graduate and professional years we have not helped—we have weakened —undergraduate education. The undergraduate program is viewed as less serious in the sense that it need achieve no mastery of a subject, since all that will be accomplished later. But the ability to work with the intellectual disciplines is the true test of a liberal education, which in that way has always been, and should be, vocational. We thus face a situation where graduate education takes longer than it ought to, could start earlier, and in other ways could frequently compress what it does—where undergraduate education is weaker for the aimlessness which it now enjoys. The system is wasteful of human lives, requiring as a matter of course too many years. And it is wasteful of economic resources at a time when there are great needs within the educational system to help out at the secondary, primary, and preprimary school levels.

In education we have much to be proud of, much to preserve. We are the beneficiaries of extraordinary efforts to make available to us and to make vital within us an intellectual tradition previously reserved for a few. Our institutions of learning in many ways are the noblest achievements of our world. If we are careless with them, if we take them for granted as though they were among the given wonders of nature, we must expect them to decline. Our generations will be held accountable for this. The decline will begin with the distortions of success. Here, as in other walks of life, we must try to renew our central purposes.

Frazier's *The Golden Bough* describes many folk customs, including those surrounding the selection and training of the youth who are to become the leaders and the teachers of the primitive community. The young men are removed from their families. They are taken away to live in a magic wood. There they live in isolation for a number of years. There they are instructed. They receive a special education. They learn a new language, new dances and verses and other accomplishments which represent the special values and knowledge of the tribe. There they are seized with a new spirit. Even in these traditional societies a reawakening and a new awareness are required. The youth are supposed, as the commentator writes, "to have become new beings in the magic wood. . . . On their return to the village they pretend to have entirely forgotten their life before they entered the wood." But this pretense, we are assured by the writer, "is not kept up beyond the period of festivities given to welcome them home" on the completion of their course. It is a great advantage for the society and for them to have had them receive this instruction; a great advantage to look with a new awareness; a great joy to welcome you home.

14

The Strategy of Truth

An address given on the occasion of the author's inauguration
as president of the University of Chicago
14 November 1968

175

I trust I will be forgiven a personal word. I approach this unlikely moment with many memories. I come to it also with understandable concern. I do not misconceive the importance of this office which has changed through the years. Rather, the goals, achievement, and tradition of this university are disturbingly impressive. Our university has had a standard of extraordinary leadership, difficult to maintain. I am grateful to Chancellor Hutchins, Chancellor Kimpton, and President Beadle for their presence today. They will understand my anxiety. It is not that we fear mistakes. Perhaps we should fear not to make them. President Hutchins in his address—given forty years ago—spoke of the university's experimental attitude, its willingness to try out ideas, to undertake new ventures, to pioneer. In some cases, he said, the contribution was to show other universities what not to do. Let me say, with rueful pride, since that time we have made many similar contributions. I hope we always will.

It is natural for this university to believe it believes in pioneering. After all, this university came into being as a pioneering first modern university, borrowing ideas from Germany and England, building upon the New England college, joining undergraduate instruction and a panoply of graduate research in what, some said, surely would be a monstrosity—all this done with middle-western enthu-

siasm and a confidence the best could be obtained
here if only it could be paid for. Much has been
written of the financial arrangements of those days,
the creative use of material resources generously
given. But the basic faith was not in material resources. The faith was in the intellectual powers of
the mind. It was considered important, more important than anything else in the world, to uncover and
understand the cultures of the past, to appreciate the
works of the mind, to penetrate the mysteries of the
universe, to know more about the environment, the
societies, and the nature of man. The university's
seriousness of purpose was proven from the first by
its insistence upon freedom of inquiry and discussion. Intellectual tests for truth made other standards irrelevant. Schools for the propagation of special points of view might exist, Harper wrote, but
they could not be called universities. The emphasis
on the need to question and reexamine, both as part
of the inquiry of research and the inquiry of teaching, established a basic unity for all of the university.
The basis of that unity underscored the relationship
between teaching and research. That unity encouraged discussion among disciplines. It supported the
individual scholar as he crossed accepted boundaries
of knowledge. It made possible—even compelled—
continuing debate concerning the place of professional, specialized, general, and liberal education
within the university. It made the university self-
critical.

"On an occasion such as this," as Mr. Kimpton
stated on a similar occasion, "the important roles are
not played by those who are present. . . . Our efforts
are given importance by the opportunities and re-

sponsibilities . . . we inherit." So I have stressed those virtues which from the beginning and until now have characterized our institution: a willingness to experiment, a commitment to the intellectual search for truth, freedom of inquiry, and a concern for the educational process as though the freedom of man depended upon it. This is our inheritance. It is an inheritance preserved and strengthened, indeed made possible, by the action and faith of many who are present today.

We meet in a time of great difficulty. The society is divided. The conditions of public discussion have changed. More people can take part and react because they can be reached. Both the numbers involved and the means of communication increase the likelihood—and certainly the powers—of distortion. The problems are complex; the limits of knowledge are agonizingly apparent in matters of public policy. Meanwhile the investigations of the social sciences have made clearer the nonrational components of human behavior. The relevance and integrity of reason are questioned at the same time as impatience emphasizes the manipulative aspects of concepts and institutions.

The outrage of this war continues.

The view of the world as it is or could be is conditioned for many by the protective walls or barriers of higher education. Formal education at both the college and graduate level is highly regarded as the gateway to success. More than 45 percent of our young people in the applicable age group are in college—an extraordinary change and, with some qualifications, an extraordinary achievement. But the joyous news that the bank of knowledge is overstuffed, and can be drawn upon only with the assistance of the latest generation of computers, adds to the impression of a technical, industrialized society in which individual thought and concern are powerless —in which basic decisions appear to have been made in other times or by other people in other places. The very idea that centers of education are for thoughtful, and therefore personal, consideration of values, and for increased understanding, is lost by those who insist that universities are mechanisms of service to be used in a variety of ways for the interests of the larger community.

There are many institutions for service in our society. Centers of learning and instruction have considerable difficulty in performing their central tasks; one may question the wisdom of assigning to them additional duties. In any event, among colleges, schools, and universities there are important differences. Our history, capacity, and objectives are not all the same. Each institution must find its own mission.

The mission of the University of Chicago is primarily the intellectual search for truth and the transmission of intellectual values. The emphasis must be on the achievement of that understanding which can be called discovery. President Beadle has spoken, as is his special right to do, of "the incomparable thrill of original discovery." He has referred to the importance of having students participate in the process through which knowledge is reaffirmed and additions to knowledge are made. This, of course, is the process of education, whatever the means used, and it applies to the dialogue as well as to the experiment. We should reaffirm the close connection between the creativity of teaching and the creativity of research. And we should reaffirm also our commitment to the way of reason, without which a university becomes a menace and a caricature.

It is of course easy to be in favor of reason. But the commitment is somewhat more demanding and difficult. President Harper in his decennial report took occasion to emphasize "that the principle of complete freedom of speech on all subjects has from the beginning been regarded as fundamental to the University of Chicago." At the same time he repeated the policy that "the University, as such, does not appear as a disputant on either side upon any public question, and . . . utterances which any professor may make in public are to be regarded as representing his opinion only." Academic freedom is stronger now than it was then. But the propriety of the corporate neutrality of the university on public policy issues having moral aspects has been seriously challenged. The position questions the power or persuasiveness of ideas in themselves, recognizes the superior authority of official certification, or places reliance on other forms of power. Perhaps the position reflects the kind of frustration described by Louis Wirth in 1936. Professor Wirth wrote: "At a time in human history like our own, when all over the world people are not merely ill at ease but are questioning the bases of social existence, the validity of their truths, and the tenability of their norms, it should become clear that there is no value apart from interest and no objectivity apart from agreement. Under such circumstances it is difficult to hold tenaciously to what one believes to be the truth in the face of dissent, and one is inclined to question the very possibility of an intellectual life. Despite the fact

that the Western world has been nourished by a tradition of hard-won intellectual freedom and integrity
for over two thousand years, men are beginning to
ask whether the struggle to achieve these was worth
the cost if so many today accept complacently the
threat to exterminate what rationality and objectivity
have been won in human affairs. The widespread de-
preciation of the value of thought, on the one hand,
and its repression, on the other, are ominous signs
of the deepening twilight of modern culture."

The issue raised is central to what a university
should be and what it should stand for. It is of course
quite true that the ideas of individual scholars in universities are not likely to immediately sway the world,
although some have had considerable effect. The tasks
which university faculty have undertaken, sometimes
within, sometimes without the universities, should
not obscure the fact that universities exist for the long
run. They are the custodians not only of the many
cultures of man, but of the rational process itself.
Universities are not neutral. They do exist for the
propagation of a special point of view: namely, the
worthwhileness of the intellectual pursuit of truth—
using man's highest powers, struggling against the ir-
revelancies which corrupt thought, and now standing
against the impatience of those who have lost faith in
reason. This view does not remove universities from
the problems of society. It does not diminish, indeed it
increases, the pressure for the creation and exchange
of ideas, popular or unpopular, which remake the
world. It does suggest that the greatest contribution
of universities will be in that liberation of the mind
which makes possible what Kenneth Clark has called
the strategy of truth. "For," as he says, "the search

for truth, while impotent without implementation in action, undergirds every other strategy in behalf of constructive social change." One would hope that this liberation of the mind would result from a liberal education at Chicago at both the undergraduate and graduate level.

One can well understand the impatience of those who prefer a different relevance of practical action. In some areas, implementation, leading to a more basic examination of consequences and meaning, has been made an appropriate part of training and research. But this may be insufficient to satisfy those who for the time being at least, and for laudable and understandable reasons, would prefer a different way of life. Nevertheless, they stay within the educational system caught by its pretense and rigidity. They feel they must stay a long time. Not only has the number of years required for formal education steadily increased as college and graduate work are treated as necessities, but the model presses for the total absorption of the student's interest either in the curriculum or in ancillary activities. We are set on a course which suggests that every young person up to the age of twenty-five, every young family really, should have an educational institution as a surrogate for the world. Quite apart from the fact that institutions of higher learning should not be surrogates for the world, the satisfaction with which this development is greeted should be tempered. This development in part is a response to distortions caused by the Selective Service System. Much of the education at the graduate level—in some areas, not all—is unnecessary, or even worse is disqualifying for professional work, as for example the undergraduate teaching for which it is required. I do not expect agreement on that and I am probably wrong. For some areas I doubt whether the extended time can be justified as a reflection of the increase in knowledge. Rather, it appears as an unimaginative response on the part of the educational system to the existence of increased leisure time within the economy. And if the goal of a college education for everyone is to be met in a way to do the most good, the purposes and ways of that education, even the period of time involved, should be reexamined. I realize this has been done before, but perhaps it will not hurt too much to take another look. What I am trying to suggest is that for those who are interested in pioneering, there is much to think about. The university is a member of many communities. We cherish the relationship with other universities. We are a member of their world community. We are also an urban university on the South Side of Chicago. In many ways through many activities various members of the university faculties and students are working within the community. We seek to be a good neighbor. Most of us are in fact neighbors. The community has much to offer us. The fact that most of our faculty live here has helped to maintain the oneness and interdisciplinary character of this institution. It has made it possible to measure the effect of new enterprises and responsibilities upon the institution as a whole. This guideline enforces self-restraint. It is, I think, of benefit both to the community and to the university. New models for pediatric care, for counseling and psychiatric assistance, and new approaches to the major problems of urban education should emerge from the endeavors which have been planned and developed with representatives of the community. These are not the only scholarly-service-training activities in which members of the faculty are engaged within the community which have significance far beyond the problems of one neighborhood and which over time may well determine the quality of life in world urban centers. The work in the complex problems of communities within the city is an encouraging continuation of historic research begun fifty years ago by the Chicago school of sociology.

In 1902 President Harper referred to the firmly established policy of the trustees "that to the faculties belongs to the fullest extent the care of educational administration." "The responsibility," he said, "for the settlement of educational questions rests with the faculty." On this policy the initial greatness of the university was built. The trustees, whether they agreed or not with particular decisions, have been the strongest advocates of this policy. And the faculty have fulfilled this responsibility, protecting on the one hand the freedom of the individual scholar, and shepherding at the same time, although not without some pain, some of the most interesting programs for both undergraduate and graduate instruction attempted in this country. I stress the position of the faculty because obviously the quality of this university rests upon them and is created by them. And the burdens upon them have increased because the conditions of education have changed. Sir Eric Ashby in a notable address at the University of Witwatersrand quoted from an essay, "The Open Universities of South Africa," as follows: "There is no substitute for the clash of mind between colleague and colleague, between teacher and student, between student and student. . . . It is here the half-formed idea may take shape, the groundless belief be shattered, the developing theory be tested. . . . It is here the controversy develops, and out of controversy, deeper understanding." Today when there is doubt and skepticism concerning the very tradition of intellectual freedom and integrity upon which the intellectual pursuit of knowledge is based, it is important that the university through its faculty meet these questions head on.

This university has indeed been fortunate in the dedication which throughout the years it has evoked. It has been surrounded by a circle of friends, who by their aspirations for the university and their own self-sacrifice have assured its pursuit of quality and its inner integrity.

I am proud to be in this place and I shall do my best.